JOHN OF THE CROSS FOR TODAY:

The Ascent

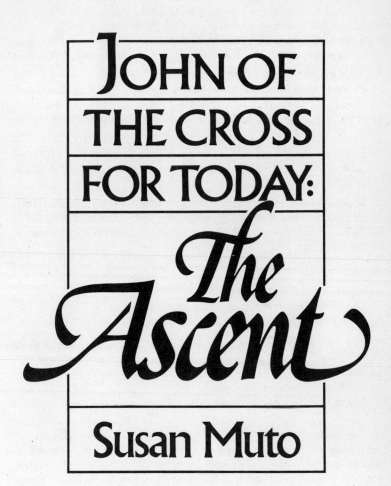

JOHN OF THE CROSS FOR TODAY:

The Ascent

Susan Muto

AVE MARIA PRESS
Notre Dame, Indiana 46556

Certain chapters of this book are based on articles and bibliographies which appeared in the following journals. They are incorporated here with the permission of *Living Prayer*, 20:1 (January-February, 1987); *Review for Religious*, 46:2 (March-April, 1987); *Envoy*, 25:1 (January-February, 1988); *Mount Carmel*, 36:1 (Spring, 1988) and 37:2 (Summer, 1989); and *Carmelite Digest*, 4:3 (Summer, 1989) and the St. John Centenary Edition (1991).

Excerpts from *The Collected Works of St. John of the Cross*, translated by Kieran Kavanaugh and Otilio Rodriguez © 1979 by Washington Province of Discalced Carmelites. ICS Publications 2131 Lincoln Road, N.E. Washington, D.C. 20002.

Scripture texts used are those found in *The Collected Works of St. John of the Cross*, trans. Kieran Kavanaugh, O.C.D., and Otilio Rodriguez, O.C.D.

Scripture texts other than those mentioned above are from THE NEW JERUSALEM BIBLE, copyright ©1985 by Darton, Longman & Todd, Ltd. and Doubleday & Company, Inc. Reprinted by permission of the publisher.

Imprimatur:
The Most Reverend Donald William Wuerl
Bishop of Pittsburgh

The nihil obstat and the imprimatur are declarations that a work is considered to be free from doctrinal or moral error. It is not implied that those who have granted the same agree with the contents, opinions or statements expressed.
Given this 18th day of June, 1990.

International Standard Book Number: 0-87793-440-1
0-87793-439-8 (pbk.)

Library of Congress Catalog Card Number: 90-84357

Cover and text design by Elizabeth J. French

Printed and bound in the United States of America.

This book is dedicated to
Adrian van Kaam, C.S.Sp., Ph.D.,
who has shown me and so many
the path of transcendence.

Contents

Chapter 1
Love's Urgent Longings

Chapter 2
Faith in Darkness

Chapter 3
To Lose Is to Gain

Chapter 4
Touched by the Transcendent

Chapter 5
Nothing Only God

Chapter 6
Spiritual Apprehensions and the Night of Faith

Acknowledgments

Throughout this book there are references to the science of formative spirituality developed so thoroughly and astutely over the years by my colleague and co-author of many books, Father Adrian van Kaam, C.S.Sp., Ph.D. His work in this field manifests a devotion to God and a clarity of mind that two of his intellectual and spiritual mentors, St. Thomas Aquinas and St. John of the Cross, have certainly inspired. I am so indebted to his guidance, teaching, friendship, and support over the years that I have chosen to dedicate this book to him.

I acknowledge as well the work of my administrative secretary at the Epiphany Association, Marilyn Russell, who faithfully typed the manuscript and monitored its completion. In truth a book happens because of the encouragement of many people and especially, in this case, of students to whom I have taught St. John's writings over the years; to editors who have published my articles; to audiences who have asked for more; and above all to my family members and friends in the Epiphany Association, whose practice of the life of the spirit inspires me daily.

I would also like to thank the Institute of Carmelite Studies in Washington, D.C. for granting me permission to cite throughout this text quotations from the *Ascent* and other writings in their superb edition of *The Collected Works of St. John of the Cross*, translated by Kieran Kavanaugh, O.C.D., and Otilio Rodriguez, O.C.D. (ICS Publications, 1979). I urge you to purchase a copy of this text and to study it and its introductions side by side with this reading. It provides essential historical background I do not need to repeat here.

To one and all who have helped to make this book a reality, I offer my sincere thanks. I ask you, too, to join me in thanking God for giving us the gift of St. John,

9

for using this small statured spiritual giant, this once obscure Spanish Carmelite, to teach us as no one before or since has about the way leading to union with God in love.

The higher he ascends
The less he understands,
Because the cloud is dark
Which lit up the night;
Whoever knows this
Remains always in unknowing
Transcending all knowledge.

—*Stanzas Concerning an*
Ecstasy Experienced
in High Contemplation

When I ascended higher
My vision was dazzled,
And the most difficult conquest
Was achieved in darkness;
But since I was seeking love
The leap I made was blind and dark
And I rose so high, so high,
That I took the prey.

—*More Stanzas Applied*
to Spiritual Things

Introduction

Two trends in contemporary life convince me that the time is ripe for a contemporary reading of *The Ascent of Mount Carmel*. The first has to do with the popularity of psychology, which can now be termed "psychologism." Average people regularly turn to this distinctive body of knowledge when they are in trouble. Abusive relations, adolescents on drugs, broken marriages, midlife burn outs — all these problems find their way into the popular media. People listen to television personalities, not faith-filled spiritual guides wise in the knowledge of classical spirituality and theology, when they want to know, practically speaking, what to do. Page after page of advice appears in print; more is broadcast on television and radio talk shows. Few, if any, readers or listeners would think of seeking guidance from a great classic like the *Ascent*. But, as I intend to show, this book can still meet the need for mentorship that led St. John to compose it, starting in 1579. It is eminently formative yet down to earth, deep yet accessible to the discerning eye, ancient yet ever new.

The advice people do receive from popular psychologism centers them first and foremost not in God but in their own powers of *self*-actualization, *self*-development, *self*-esteem, *self*-control, and *self*-fulfillment. Psychologism is incredibly *self*-, not God-, centered. It is rooted in the basic illusion of *hubris*, in the deceptive, pride-filled mentality that *I* or *we* alone can mold, manage, and maintain our "act" without reference to a Higher Power. The self-alone myth is based on so false a premise that it inevitably self-destructs. At this juncture the second trend, with its inherent dangers and deceptions, may arise. With it comes another major reason why we need to read in a contemporary manner books as basic and illuminating as the *Ascent-Dark Night*.

People who say they have seen it all, done it all, and expended a great deal of time, money, and effort to find themselves may discover instead that they have not reached self-fulfillment at all, only ego-desperation. In other words, lacking any real interiority to turn to when life deals out a harsh hand in the form of sickness, unemployment, failure, or addiction, people know they cannot do it alone. Many at this point go through a spiritual awakening. They may find themselves at last in affective contact with the living God. Many experience sudden, powerful graces leading to conversion. Some come to this turning point more slowly through formation counseling, group therapy, private or common spiritual direction. Whatever access route to God grace provides, all agree that theirs has been a kind of prodigal son or daughter experience of returning to the house of a forgiving host, full of divine mercy and love.

These journeys inward may be accompanied by remarkable, at times even extraordinary, consolations, spiritual touches, delights, visions, and feelings. One is on a real "high," mystically and personally, on a mountaintop of love and wholeness from which one admittedly does not want to depart. The spiritually awakened person desires in the worst way to perpetuate this experience. As a result, she or he may search for new and higher mountaintops, not realizing that spirituality proper actually begins in the valley of everyday living.

Such a person needs to hear the sober counsel contained in the *Ascent*. Others who have undergone awakening experiences may know intuitively that they are but an invitation to go deeper. They are not the end, merely the pristine beginning, of the journey to union with God. For them, too, the *Ascent* is a true beginner's book. It starts exactly at the point where God begins to wean the soul away from divine consolations toward an in-depth relationship with the God who consoles.

The *Ascent* is St. John's own commentary on his magnificent poem, the *Dark Night*. The commentary continues in a second book of that title, which takes the pilgrim soul a significant step further on the journey to God, into the realm of pure receptive contemplation. This book also provides an essential road map for people more advanced in the life of the spirit. It merits its own companion text in due course.

In my opinion the *Ascent* contains in its timeless, timely fashion the wisdom people need to hear, especially if they have reached one or the other stage of ego-desperation and if they have undergone an initial awakening experience. Now they wonder, as many do, where do we go from here? St. John has the answer. Four hundred years after his death, he is the man of the hour. Let us begin our considerations by slowly and reflectively reading his wonderful poem in its entirety.

The Dark Night

One dark night
Fired with love's urgent longings
— Ah, the sheer grace! —
I went out unseen,
My house being now all stilled.

In darkness, and secure,
By the secret ladder, disguised,
— Ah, the sheer grace! —
In darkness and concealment,
My house being now all stilled;

On that glad night,
In secret, for no one saw me,
Nor did I look at anything,
With no other light or guide
Than the one that burned in my heart;

14

This guided me
More surely than the light of noon
To where He waited for me
— Him I knew so well —
In a place where no one else appeared.

O guiding night!
O night more lovely than the dawn!
O night that has united
The Lover with His beloved,
Transforming the beloved in her Lover.

Upon my flowering breast
Which I kept wholly for Him alone,
There He lay sleeping,
And I caressing Him
There in the breeze from the fanning cedars.

When the breeze blew from the turret
Parting His hair,
He wounded my neck
With His gentle hand,
Suspending all my senses.

I abandoned and forgot myself,
Laying my face on my Beloved;
All things ceased; I went out from myself,
Leaving my cares
Forgotten among the lilies.*

---

*All quotes, cited by title, book, paragraph and/or number, can
be found in *The Collected Works of St. John of the Cross*, trans. Kieran
Kavanaugh, O.C.D., and Otilio Rodriguez, O.C.D. (Washington, D.C.:
Institute of Carmelite Studies, 1979). This poem in Spanish with the
English translation appears on pp. 711–712 of this edition.

1

Love's Urgent Longings

The Active Night of the Senses
(Book One, Chapters 1 to 15, of the *Ascent*)

Segovia. I had longed to see the chapel at the Carmelite convent where the remains of the saint whose words had for so long touched and formed my inner life were accorded proper honor. Now, at last I was in Spain, in this beautiful historical place, the final stop on my sabbatical trip. I knew that I was standing on sacred ground the minute I entered the chapel with its life-size murals depicting scenes from the travels and encounters of St. John and St. Teresa of Avila. Her name is as known in the region today as it was in her time. St. John was and remains more obscure.

For whatever reason, perhaps it was siesta, the chapel was empty, yet in the silence I sensed a presence. So this is *nada*, I said to myself, the nothingness that is all. Then my eyes began to focus on the magnificent altarpiece depicting in vivid hues the journey from twilight, to the heart of darkness where faith alone is our guide, to the first faint glimmer of dawn. In primary colors — the greys and blacks of purification, the whites and yellows of illumination, the reds and purples of union — the artist drew the movement of the soul from the pits of selfishness to the pinnacle of selflessness, from desolation to divine consummation. The lights and shadows of this superb work of art seemed to suspend my senses in a moment of awe. At journey's end, I knew I had just begun to understand the truths this beloved master has to teach.

Preparing for the Journey

The first book of the *Ascent* presupposes that we have reached a stage in our spiritual life where we are ready to be led by God beyond the beginnings of prayer to the deeper regions of divine intimacy. St. John is writing for "advanced" beginners and persons already proficient in the virtues of detachment, humility, and charity. In other words, he is writing for people who have a "self" to lose. It is in fact dangerous to read St. John if we have not tasted a certain degree of success mingled with a good dose of self-esteem. It is impossible to lose a self we do not have. People can become quite sick if they try to annihilate what does not exist. To enjoy the *Ascent*, it is essential to have reached what I like to call the "so what" moment. So *I* have tried it all, done it all, owned or imagined owning it all—so what? *I'm* still not happy, *I* long for more, *I* need God as never before. Now we are ready to proceed as advanced beginners, moving with St. John to a new, transcendent plane of self-transformation.

The aim of Book One is threefold: to help us liberate our deepest self from the burden of worldly, inordinate attachments; to share the knowledge St. John has gathered through his reading, experience of prayer, and direction of others about the obstacles we can expect to encounter; and to describe in concrete detail how we can find the way to live in the freedom of spirit necessary for divine union.

In the prologue to Book One, the saint says he has been guided on this journey above all by "love's urgent longings," by the desire for God. Essential also is the wisdom provided by sacred scripture and the doctrine of the church. He targets immediately two main hindrances to advancement: inadequate direction and inadequate discernment. Spiritual directors, lacking sufficient knowledge and experience of what is happening to persons after their awakening may unwittingly encourage them to continue in their old ways. This is "bad" direction.

> God gives many souls the talent and grace for advancing, and should they desire to make the effort they would arrive at this high state. And so it is sad to see them continue in their lowly method of communion with God because they do not want or know how to advance, or because they receive no direction on breaking away from the methods of beginners (AMC, I, Prologue [3]).

Failing to understand that God is the author of this enlightenment, ill-prepared directors may urge awakened persons to return to former ways of prayer, to make many general confessions, but not to advance further. This is bad discernment. Those so counseled may neither know where to go from here nor whether they even want to advance. Should the Lord himself come to them, the question remains: Will they be willing to adapt themselves to his work? Both the director and those directed fail to realize that now is not the time for the activity of the past:

> Indeed it is a period for leaving these persons alone in the purgation God is working in them, a time to give comfort and encouragement that they may desire to endure this suffering as long as God wills, for until then, no remedy — whatever the soul does, or the confessor says — is adequate (AMC, I, Prologue [5]).

Following these observations, St. John begins in chapters one and two to explain the imagery of the "night"

that will guide us on our journey. Early evening or twilight marks the point of departure, the time of purgation,
when we experience deprivations in the area of worldly
pleasures, possessions, and powers. As we begin to mortify these attachments, we may be drawn by grace still
deeper into the night — to the midnight hour, dense and
dark, where the only means of ascent is faith. Intellect,
memory, and will are deprived of their normal ways
of remembering and loving so that we may be made
ready for the secret and intimate self-communications of
God. The night eventually gives way to daybreak, to the
dawn, symbolizing the point of God's arrival, when the
lover is transformed into perfect union with her Beloved.

These phases of the night encompass the threefold
path of purgation, illumination, and union, not as something accomplished once and for all in linear fashion,
but as an ongoing cycle of deprivation, restoration, and
graced transformation. One discovers through the nights
of sense and spirit that no thing, concept, image or idea
can fulfill our infinite desire for God.

Entering the Night

The point of chapter three is to identify the first cause
of this night as the "privation" or deprivation of per-
verted desires or appetites. Perhaps this is St. John's
way of explaining control of the pleasure principle as a
necessary condition for spiritual deepening. This control
actually entails a rechanneling of vital energies so that
they flow from and return to their transcendent source.
We must go through this "night" in order to restore equi-
librium. Life has been thrown off balance by excessive
attachment to persons, things, and events in isolation
from their divine source.

St. John believes that all creation is good; nothing is
evil in itself. Ideally we ought to proceed from the manifestations of God to the Mystery from whence creation

flows forth. In reality, due to the spiritual blindness im-
posed by original sin, we cling frantically to the gratification of vital needs, to the satisfaction of functional
ambitions. We tend to make persons or things ultimate
sources of pleasure or possession. They become idols or
ends in themselves. The result of not entering the night
of sense deprivation is an increase in formation ignorance, described by Adrian van Kaam as forgetfulness
of our true transcendent nature, of our distinctively human or spiritual potency.

We need the "night" to reawaken our capacity to
remember the transcendent in our sense perception of
things. We are not to stay only on the surface of life but
to behold in faith its depth dimension. By turning the
senses of hearing, seeing, smelling, tasting, and touching
away from the objects of their desire as ultimate, we are
paradoxically freeing our powers of apprehension of the
Holy. In short, "Since the things of the world cannot enter the soul, they are not in themselves an encumbrance
or harm to it; rather, it is the will and appetite dwelling
within it that causes the damage" (AMC, I, 3 [4]).

St. John suggests in chapters four and five three essential steps to follow, in a word, *remembrance, comparison,*
and *renunciation.*

To be freed from the idle/idol illusion of being satisfied with anything less than God, we must strive to remember the right relation between creation and Creator.
Curiously enough, this re-membering has to do with
dis-membering. To dis-member a thing as ultimate is to
re-member it as dependent on God. Painful as such detachment may be, it helps us to appreciate things much
more as gifts of God. By contrast, one who is clothed
in these affections (versus dis-membered) will be "incapable of the enlightenment and dominating fullness
of God's pure and simple light, unless he rejects them"
(AMC, I, 4 [1]). Harsh as it may sound, St. John holds

firm to his conviction that the light of divine union cannot be established in the soul until excessive affections are eradicated. In other words, when we temper our idolizing desire to seek gratification and to possess things outside of God, we can begin to appreciate them as they are in their pristine origin and beauty. In this way we move from a posture of control to one of letting be, from an attitude of calculation to one of compassion.

A second step is to compare the finite, limited nature of things to the "how much more" of the Infinite. The Sea of Galilee compared to the sea of God's love is like a drop of water compared to the Pacific Ocean. Creatures, however beautiful, elegant, and abundant they may be, compared to their Creator, are as darkness to light, as coarseness to grace, as ignorance to ability.

Through this exercise in comparison, St. John introduces us to the reality principle, to the art of seeing things as they really are in their limited value as pointers to the Limitless. Through this comparison, we are able to temper the tendency to make a "little beyond" into the "Great Beyond." We are less prone to invest in something finite the fullness of the Infinite. In this light, we are able to read chapter four as a litany of praise to our Creator God:

> All the being of creatures compared with the infinite being of God is nothing. . . . All the beauty of creatures compared with the infinite Beauty of God is supreme ugliness. . . . All the grace and elegance of creatures compared with God's grace is utter coarseness and crudity . . . (*AMC*, I, 4 [4]).

St. John would agree with St. Paul that the wisdom of this world is mere foolishness in God's sight (1 Cor 3:19). These statements do not intend that we reject creaturely being, beauty, grace, and ability as bad, but that we place these attributes in their proper relation to God. All will pass away, not God's word. Creaturely qualities,

no matter how rich, are ultimately poor in comparison
to the being, elegance, and wisdom of God. Our hope
resides not in this or that momentary pleasure or possession but in God alone.

If the first step out of illusion is to remember our nothingness without God, then the second step is to compare
eternal truth with whatever is temporal. The promise
God makes to us is more trustworthy than any stopping
place on the path of formation. Thus it is up to us to
keep running the race to the end, not to rest ultimately
in anything but God. As St. Augustine confesses, our
hearts are restless until they rest in God. Again, to quote
St. John:

> All the sovereignty and freedom of the world com-
> pared with the freedom and sovereignty of the Spirit
> of God is utter slavery, anguish, and captivity. . . . All
> the delights and satisfactions of the will in the things
> of the world in contrast to all the delight that is God
> is intense suffering, torment, and bitterness. . . . All
> the wealth and glory of creation compared with the
> wealth that is God is utter poverty and misery in the
> Lord's sight (AMC, I, 4 [6 and 7]).

The third step, as suggested in chapter five, is the most
radical. St. John says that total renunciation is the condition for the possibility of transformation. Here paradox
prevails. Just as knowing is only possible in unknowing,
so freedom of spirit or liberation is the result of detachment or renunciation. This kenotic experience does not
happen once and for all; it demands habitual effort in co-
operation with the graces God bestows. No compromise
is possible now:

> The road and ascent to God, then, necessarily de-
> mands a habitual effort to renounce and mortify the
> appetites; the sooner this mortification is achieved, the
> sooner the soul reaches the top. But until the appetites
> are eliminated, a person will not arrive, no matter how

much virtue he practices. For he will fail to acquire perfect virtue, which lies in keeping the soul empty, naked and purified of every appetite (*AMC*, I, 5 [6]).

If we desire to climb the summit of the mount, to become "an altar for the offering of a sacrifice of pure love and praise," we must strive to accomplish three tasks. First, we must "cast out strange gods," meaning that we have to let go of any affections and attachments that tend to alienate us from God; secondly, we must purify ourselves of their residue through habitual denial (saying *no* for the sake of a greater *yes*). As often as we fail to do so, we must return to God through habitual, confident repentance, trusting that God's mercy responds with motherly tenderness to our misery. Thirdly, we must take on a "change of garments," meaning that we must be clothed in a new understanding of God, in a new love of God in God. In this way, we move from ignorance of who we really are to acceptance of our being made in the form and likeness of God, in St. John's words, "his worthy dwelling." In this quest there is only one appetite God permits and wants. It is "the desire for the perfect fulfillment of his law and the carrying of his cross" (*AMC*, I, 5 [8]).

Detrimental Effects of Inordinate Attachment

Having reflected on the meaning and demands of total renunciation and the liberation it allows, St. John meditates in chapters six to ten on the harms appetites or inordinate desires engender in the soul. There are two main areas of harm: One is privative, which involves an aversion from God; the other positive, which corresponds to a turning toward creatures. In general, all unruly appetites deprive us of God's Spirit. Any excessive attachment to a created thing renders us less capable of soaring free to God.

St. John relies for his reasoning on the philosophical principle that two contraries cannot coexist in the same person. Therefore, "Since love of God and attachment to creatures are contraries, they cannot coexist in the same will" (*AMC*, I, 6 [1]). Rather than accept our privilege as children of God to eat at his table, we act like dogs who must eat the crumbs that fall to the floor. We refuse to rise from the "crumbs" of creatures to the uncreated Spirit of the Father. It stands to reason that "this un-created fullness cannot find entry to a soul until this other hunger caused by the desires is expelled" (*AMC*, I, 6 [3]).

As to the second harm, which is positive, we must realize that numerous impediments are wrought in the soul by untamed appetites, the most obvious of these be-ing that they weary, torment, darken, defile, and weaken the true seeker. Our spiritual life suffers in the first place because these appetites weary and tire us to death. St. John compares them to restless, discontented chil-dren, whose mothers wear out in their effort to please them. Satisfied at one moment, these discontents de-mand more attention the next. The more their mother tries to quiet their cravings, the more demanding they become. She in turn feels increasingly agitated, disturbed, and fatigued. Like the impulse governing physical hunger or sexual need, so appetites in general are stirred to satisfy themselves endlessly. St. John makes this analogy:

> Just as a lover is wearied and depressed when on a longed-for day his opportunity is frustrated, so is a man wearied and tired by all his appetites and their fulfillment, because the fulfillment only causes more hunger and emptiness. An appetite, as they say, is like a fire that blazes up when wood is thrown on it, but necessarily dies out when the wood is consumed (*AMC*, I, 6 [6]).

Such desires make it impossible for us to live in longing for God alone. It is as if we keep looking for heaven on earth. We become ready victims of illusory promises of fulfillment. We give in to the pressures of consumerism. The sad reward is discontent. We have turned unwittingly from God, who alone can satisfy us, to things that inevitably disappoint.

These inordinate appetites not only wear us out; they also torment us. They gnaw at us mercilessly, as if we were bound by tight cords or tortured on a rack. The torment is likened to that being endured by a person who is lying naked on a bed of thorns and nails. In pain, he knows no peace. Sipping water, he is still thirsty. When the cord of desires tightens around us, when the possessions we cling to possess us, we cannot enjoy the liberation of the children of God. Instead of surrendering our will to God, we lose our peace in wasted efforts.

> This movement toward abundance is a departure from the pleasures of creatures, because the creature torments, while the Spirit of God refreshes. Accordingly, God calls us through St. Matthew . . . as though He were to say: All you going about tormented, afflicted, and weighed down by your cares and appetites, depart from them, come to me and I will refresh you; and you will find the rest for your souls that the desires take away from you (Mt 11:28–29) (*AMC*, I, 7 [4]).

Self-centered desires blind us. It is as if we are living behind a cloudy pane of glass that blocks out the bright sunshine. We see only a hazy image of things — not things as they really are. Due to this blindness, it is impossible for us to think clearly. It is as if the powers of our transcendent mind are dulled by the excessive demands of the vital or functional spheres. Both natural reason and supernatural wisdom grow dark. When the intellect is obscured, the will becomes weak, the memory disordered. The desire for constant pleasure or sensual stimulation makes reflective living a virtual impossibility. Things go from bad to worse because the mind is incapable of receiving the illumination of God's wisdom; the will cannot embrace the pure love of God; the memory lessens its capacity for the impression of God's serene image upon it.

Unless these blinding desires are mortified, we cannot advance on the way of union. Once unruly appetites take over, they decrease our appraisal powers. We react on impulse, out of tune with the Christ-form in the core of our being. Released instead are the counterfeit forms of concupiscence and pride. No amount of penance can overcome this darkness if we do not strive to root out the source of the trouble — the blinding blockage of inordinate desires. They are like a cataract on the eye or specks of dust in it. Until they are removed, they obstruct vision. One way or another, in this life or in the next, these appetites have to be chastised and corrected. They have to undergo purgation before any steady progress in the spiritual life can take place. St. John laments this condition of formation ignorance in language reminiscent of the words of the prophets:

> Oh, if men but knew what a treasure of divine light this blindness caused by their affections and appetites deprives them of, and the number of misfortunes and evils these appetites occasion each day when left unmortified! ... At every step we mistake evil for good and good for evil. This is peculiar to our nature. But what will happen if appetite is added to our natural darkness? ... We have felt our way along the way as though blind, we have groped as if without eyes, and our blindness has reached the point that we stumble along in broad daylight as though walking in the dark (*AMC*, I, 8, [6–7]).

Blind desires stain and defile the soul, bringing it into bondage under the autarchic pride-form and blackening the beauty of the Christ-form we are called to release. We are like someone who is stained by pitch or blacker than coal. Yet our destiny is to be whiter than snow because the soul remains in substantial union with God. It "possesses in its natural being the perfection that God bestowed when creating it," even though in its rational being it is full of the "defilements" described here. We cannot grow in Christ-likeness without formative detachment. The tragedy is that these inclinations keep us away from the peace God is drawing us toward. Incredible as it may sound:

> One inordinate appetite alone . . . suffices to make a soul so captive, dirty, and unsightly that until the appetite is purified the soul is incapable of conformity with God in union. This is true even though there may be no matter for mortal sin in the appetite. What then will be the ugliness of a soul entirely disordered in its passions and surrendered to its appetites? How far it will be from God and his purity! (*AMC*, I, 9 [3]).

It follows that all three faculties of the soul are affected by this kind of attachment. Just as one bad spot spoils an entire garment, so intellect, memory, and will are defiled by disordered desires.

The end result is that such desires render us lukewarm, spiritually speaking. Appetites that go unmortified eventually sap the soul of the strength it needs to persevere in the practice of virtue. In this weakened state, ours is an on-again, off-again spirituality. We are usually overdependent on consolations and only sporadically attracted to steady discipline. Appetites, as it were, divide and conquer us, whereas asceticism unites our inner faculties and makes us stronger.

Lacking this discipline, we feel scattered. Our faith is easily challenged. We may be open targets for exalted schemes and projects that promise salvation. We would like to master God rather than allowing God to master us. What matters most is not God's will but our own interpretation of the easy way.

Without purgation and ongoing appraisal of the direction of our spiritual life, self-gratification, not God, becomes our center. As far as St. John is concerned, this would be hell on earth. Instead of concentrating on strengthening the practice of virtue, we care only about satisfying our desires. Little wonder, then, that they rob us of what we already have. Unmortified appetites result in killing our relationship with God. Because we did not put them gently but firmly to death, they live on to kill us. For what difference does it make if we win the whole world and lose our soul?

Three "Appetites" That Cause Harm

Having spelled out in vivid detail the privative and positive effects inordinate attachments can cause in the soul, St. John explains again in chapters eleven and twelve what kinds of appetites are most detrimental. He distinguishes three sources, moving from the least to the most harmful. These are the natural, the semivoluntary, and the voluntary.

Natural movements, as for example an attraction to good music, are of little or no hindrance to the attainment of union, provided we do not make them the only focus of our attention. Because we are a body-mind-spirit unity, because we are born with certain givens in the realm of temperament, disposition, and talent, it is impossible to eradicate natural appetites in this life. Were we to attempt to do so, our efforts would most likely be deformative. These movements go hand in hand with our creatureliness. We can experience, for instance, a hunger pang, and yet be free in the rational part of our being from the desire for food if we are participating at the moment in a period of fasting. These stirrings can even be found in persons who are simultaneously experiencing intense union of will in the prayer of quiet.

Natural appetites may actually be present in the sensory part of the soul, yet the superior part pays no attention to them, just as there can be foam on the ocean's surface and calm underneath the sea. One may even become aware of certain sexual impulses without moving away from absorption in God in the center of one's soul. As long as we pay no attention to them — letting these feelings buzz in and out like flies but not stopping to swat them — we need not be overly concerned about them.

Such is not the case with desires that lead to venial sin or those that may entail serious mortal sin. Once we consent to natural movements or temptations, we can be caught forthwith in imperfections that run contrary to God's will. If we are to reach the perfection of union with God in love, it is obvious that we must be freed from every appetite, however slight. We must have the strength in the face of temptation to refuse consent. There is a difference between "advertence" or knowingly falling into imperfection, and "inadvertence" or falling without much knowledge or control of the matter. The latter constitute the semivoluntary sins of which it is said that the just man will fall seven times a day and rise up again.

The real stumbling block resides in the voluntary appetites. Any one of these, even the most trifling, is sufficient to impede union. Especially problematic are "habitual appetites." Scattered acts rooted in diverse desires are less of a hindrance. While these are not yet entrenched habits, the soul must be liberated from them since they proceed from and may lead to habitual imperfection. Habitual, voluntary imperfections that are not completely mortified not only stand in the way

of divine union; they block spiritual progress as such.
St. John gives some examples of what he means by habitual imperfections or deformed dispositions that prevent one from responding fully and freely to the call of
God's love:

> . . . the common habit of loquacity; a small attachment
> one never really desires to conquer, for example, to
> a person, to clothing, to a book or a cell, or to the
> way food is prepared, and to other trifling conver-
> sations. . . . Any of these habitual imperfections, and
> attachment to them, causes as much harm to an indi-
> vidual as would the daily commission of many other
> imperfections (*AMC*, I, 11 [4]).

Harsh as it may sound, St. John will not compromise
his conviction that such attachments, however trifling
they may seem, will make it impossible in the long run
for one to progress in perfection. Something as simple as
insisting on the same place in a church pew can hinder
the spiritual flight the saint is talking about. The point is:

> It makes little difference whether a bird is tied by a
> thin thread or by a cord. For even if tied by thread, the
> bird will be prevented from taking off just as surely
> as if it were tied by cord — that is, it will be im-
> peded from flight as long as it does not break the
> thread. . . . This is the lot of a man who is attached to
> something, no matter how much virtue he has he will
> not reach the freedom of divine union (*AMC*, I, 11 [4]).

In one text after another, St. John comes back to this issue. How regrettable that a soul ladened like a rich vessel
with the wealth of good deeds, spiritual exercises, and
virtues never leaves port because one lacks the courage
to break the rope of a little satisfaction, attachment, or
affection. God gives us the power to sever stronger cords
while we cling to some childish act or thing God asks us
to overcome for the sake of love. Not only do we fail to
advance; we even turn back for something that amounts

to no more than a thread or a hair. "Everyone knows that not to go forward on this road is to turn back, and not to gain ground is to lose."

The goal of union demands that we continually mortify our appetites rather than indulge them. How can a log of wood be transformed into fire if a single degree of heat is lacking to its preparation? Similarly, it is St. John's contention that the soul "will not be transformed in God even if it has only one imperfection." This is so because a person has only one will, and if this is encumbered or occupied by anything, it will not possess the freedom, solitude, and purity requisite for divine transformation.

Returning to the topic of the kinds of harm the appetites can cause in the soul, St. John explains that, in regard to privative evil, only the voluntary appetites can completely deprive the soul of grace in this life and glory in the next. In respect to the positive evils (weariness, torment, blindness, defilement, weakness) the degree of harm depends on whether the appetite leads to mortal or venial sin, whether it is voluntary or semivoluntary. The harm caused by each appetite can be direct or indirect. For example, vainglory positively harms the soul in all the ways mentioned, but it most principally darkens and blinds it. The point to keep in mind is that all these evils together oppose the acts of virtue that generate contrary and corrective effects.

A virtuous act produces mildness, peace, comfort, light, purity, and strength; an inordinate appetite brings with it division, depletion, and general disruption. In short: "Through the practice of one virtue all the virtues grow, and similarly, through an increase in one vice, all the vices and their effects grow" (*AMC*, I, 12 [5]). We all know from experience that "the appetite when satisfied seems sweet and pleasant, but eventually the sour effect is felt." Think of that overstuffed feeling after a too rich meal! If and when we allow ourselves to be

carried away by our appetites, the bitter effect of losing
ourselves in vitalistic feelings or functionalistic preoc-
cupations is inevitable. Such is not the case with the
natural, involuntary appetites. Though disturbances in
this realm may seem to weaken our resolve, the actual
resistance of them has the opposite effect. In this struggle one wins strength, purity, and many other blessings,
for as was said by St. Paul: "Power is at full strength in
weakness" (2 Cor 12:9). Since it is the voluntary appetites
that bring on all these evils, the chief concern of spiritual
directors ought to be to help directees in the "immediate
mortification of every appetite." Nothing less than this
emptiness will liberate them.

Counsels That Ensure Progress

The oft-quoted thirteenth chapter of Book One delin-
eates some counsels pertaining to the active night of the
senses or how to overcome inordinate attachments and
begin to make progress on the path to spiritual maturity.
This very action is dependent on the "already-thereness"
of God's grace, which prompts one to enter this night in
the first place and thereby to remain open to the passive
way in which God accomplishes this work in us. What
is this "abridged method" that leads us from nothing
to everything, from emptiness to fullness, from renunciation to liberation, from being bound to soaring free?
It proceeds in a series of steps, which I shall summarize here.

First and foremost is the habitual desire to imitate
Christ in all of one's deeds. Nothing is more important
on the road to perfection than bringing our lives into
conformity with Christ's. This implies ongoing reading
(lectio continua) of the scriptures together with slowed
down, concentrated study or lectio divina. Knowing
Christ through his words and actions, we can better emulate his attitudes in our own situation, thus drawing

our entire existence more and more into union and communion with him.

It follows that to succeed in this quest of conformity to Christ, we need to renounce by and large sensory satisfactions that do not give sufficient honor and glory to God. We cannot do so on the basis of will power alone; our motivation must emerge not from fear but from love of Jesus, whose one desire was to fulfill the Father's will, which he called "his meat and food" (Jn 4:34). What does this decision mean concretely? The answer resides in the phrase "do not desire." By it St. John means do not desire to hear, look upon, act, or take pleasure in anything that is unrelated to the service and worship of God. St. John would never be against enjoying good music, if we have an ear for it, or appreciating the beauty of nature or art, or delivering or hearing a good homily. What bothers him is the tendency to stop at the sensual level instead of going through and beyond it to the sacred mystery to which it points. Being human, we cannot help but experience satisfaction in these sensory goods. The key to spiritual progress is not to desire this gratification as such but to desire mainly the God who gratifies. By this method, we leave the senses, as it were, in darkness and, from the spiritual point of view, "gain a great deal in a short time."

Such vigilance, perhaps understood as purity or singleness of heart, leads to a tranquilizing or harmonizing of the natural passions of joy, hope, fear, and sorrow — four emotions that constitute the basis of the active purgation of the will by love in Book III, chapter sixteen and following, of the *Ascent*. Here it suffices for St. John to present a few maxims, a first formula, as it were, for pacifying these passions while practicing many virtues. What we are pacifying again is the *passion for* or the *inordinate attachment to* satisfactions that are self-centered; expectations that are willful; anxieties rooted in our search for security; and depressions due to lack of control when things do not go our way. Only if we understand this point can we accept the wisdom contained in these well-known maxims:

> Endeavor to be inclined always:
> not to the easiest, but to the most difficult;
> not to the most delightful, but to the harshest;
> not to the most gratifying, but to the less pleasant;
> not to what means rest for you, but to hard work;
> not to the consoling, but to the unconsoling;
> not to the most, but to the least;
> not to the highest and most precious, but to the lowest and most despised;
> not to wanting something, but to wanting nothing;
> do not go about looking for the best of temporal things, but
> for the worst,
> and desire to enter into complete nudity, emptiness and poverty in everything in the world (*AMC*, I, 13 [6]).

This passage may seem life-denying, even slightly masochistic, and certainly discouraging, if we overlook the crucial phrase at the beginning, which says, "*Endeavor* to be inclined always . . ." This is the same as saying "strive," "try," "foster the inclination" to develop that sixth sense that guides a true follower of Christ not to give in to egocentricity but willingly to take up the cross for Christ's sake. A worthy goal is to become proficient in detecting the lure of the pride-form. Christ chose the "narrow way," which was, by human standards, most difficult, harsh, and unpleasant. He strove so hard to accomplish our salvation that he had nowhere to rest his head. His agony was without consolation. He was numbered among the least, when his only desire was to fulfill the Father's will. If we want to walk with him, we too must practice poverty of spirit, emptying ourselves of whatever poses a hindrance to humility.

In these counsels St. John indicates concretely how
we are to accomplish the imitation of Christ. Paradoxically, by entering into *nothingness*, we enter into *noth-
ing-butness* — for nothing but God will satisfy our
restless hearts. Practiced with order and discretion, mortifications can facilitate our living in faithfulness to our
unique call. What is easiest and what is most difficult
depends, of course, on who we are. It may be easiest
for a research scientist not to spend tedious hours in
his laboratory looking for formulas that will benefit human health when he would rather be on the golf course.
Hence, what is difficult and to be done for Christ by
the scientist is to maintain his place in the lab, utilizing to the full his God-given talents. For another person,
the most difficult chore may be to overcome her shyness
and meet colleagues on the golf course, to temper her
workaholic tendency and relax for a change. Mortification, in other words, has to be "in sync" with who we
are. To engage in what Adrian van Kaam calls "syntonic
mortification," we must exercise the appraisal powers of
our transcendent mind and will. Supporting these faculties and guaranteeing prudence is the basic counsel,
"Endeavor to be inclined always" to imitate Christ and
to be ready to do what is most consonant with our call
to discipleship.

This commitment will inevitably lead us through the
"narrow gate" of the night of the senses. We have to die
to the old, unredeemed, fleshy pride-form, the "pride
of life," as St. John calls it. "Concupiscence" reigns in
the world as separated from God and gives rise to all
the appetites. We are to act with contempt for the pride-
form, for nothing short of a complete rejection of pride
will ready us to follow Christ. A contemptuous *no* for
the sake of a greater *yes* enables us in effect to say *no*
to the deception that we are in charge of our destiny.
Only if we grow strong in Christ can we be ready to

face the greater struggle to come in the dark night of
the spirit, where our only guide is faith. To follow these
counsels is thus an essential, preliminary step toward
the attainment of formation freedom. Only if we desire
nothing can God give us everything.

In summary, to mortify "the concupiscence of the
flesh" means to cease allowing any lesser God to become a substitute for the transcendent. To mortify "the
concupiscence of the eyes" means to cease allowing our
penchant for envious competition and ego-control to
dominate our existence. And, ultimately, to mortify the
"pride of life" means to root out the source of our trouble
by becoming servants of the Most High.

St. John's basic instructions for climbing to the summit
of the mount, to a state of "high union," are unforgettable:

> To reach satisfaction in all
>   desire its possession in nothing.
> To come to possess all
>   desire the possession of nothing.
> To arrive at being all
>   desire to be nothing.
> To come to the knowledge of all
>   desire the knowledge of nothing.
> To come to the pleasure you have not
>   you must go by a way in which you enjoy not.
> To come to the knowledge you have not
>   you must go by a way in which you know not.
> To come to the possession you have not
>   you must go by a way in which you possess not.
> To come to be what you are not
>   you must go by a way in which you are not.
> For to go from all to the All
>   you must deny yourself of all in all
> And when you come to the possession of the all
>   you must possess it without wanting anything.
> Because if you desire to have something in all
>   your treasure in God is not purely your all.

> In this nakedness the spirit finds
>   its quietude and rest.
> For in coveting nothing,
>   nothing raises it up
>   and nothing weighs it down,
>   because it is in the center of its humility.
> When it covets something
>   in this very desire it is wearied.
>   (*AMC*, I, 13 [11])

What St. John is saying in these remarkable verses is that we will reach the highest state of harmony and freedom only if we desire *nothing but God*. We will know all that we need to know only if we remember that we are *no-thing*. We are children of God, emerging from and returning to our Divine Ground, with all the dignity that essential, unique call affords even the most despised.

Thus if we seek a pleasure higher than any vital stimulation can give, if we long for an understanding greater than any reason can reach, if we want to possess more than any collection of material or spiritual goods can yield, if we want to be who we most deeply are, then we must trust in the incomprehensible, divine mystery of God that always escapes our urge to master it. To be this free we must go by a way in which our pride-form is not, in which our ego-functional self is increasingly "naughted," so that Christ can live in us. Every time we turn toward some thing, person, or event as ultimate or absolute, we turn away from the God of all. We cease to cast ourselves upon God's mercy, forgiveness, love. To go from the all (God's gifts everywhere) to the All (God himself), we must abandon the illusion that the All can be found or contained in any one thing. God is beyond every idol we create. To possess God, we must cease wanting anything but God; otherwise our desire will not be wholly in God as our all.

Only in this emptiness can we experience equanimity. By desiring only God's will in adversity and prosperity, in consolation and desolation, nothing else can raise us up, nothing else can weigh us down. It is a blessed state to live in the center of our humility, to walk graciously in the truth of who we are. To covet something produces the opposite effect: weariness and torment. Little wonder the God who loves us stirs up the urgent longings that lead to lasting union.

Book One closes with two short chapters that provide a transition to Book Two. The result of this initial purgation of the appetites is a more intense enkindling of the love of God above all other loves. Our motivation for giving up excessive attachments must be based neither on fear of punishment nor on the presumption of merit but on the freedom to choose a higher good. "By finding his satisfaction and strength in this love, a man will have the courage and constancy to deny readily all other appetites" (*AMC*, I, 14 [2]).

Since sensory appetites are always in a state of "craving," spiritual desires must be fired with other more "urgent longings." Lacking this transcendence dynamic, the soul will not be able to overcome the yoke of absolutized impulses and ambitions (what St. John calls the "yoke of nature"), not by rejecting these things as such but by denying the desire for them as if they could provide the fulfillment God alone can offer.

St. John plans to deal with these matters more fully in upcoming books on the active night of the spirit in which he will discuss the purification of the spiritual faculties of intellect, memory, and will by, respectively, faith, hope, and love. To have passed through the night of sense mortification, the night in which the house of self-will is stilled, is itself a "sheer grace." God's grace, his always active implicit and explicit embrace of love, has released us already from the prison of "fallenness." Our sinful self is still subject to unruly appetites. Hence, to be liberated from this bondage, to be impeded by neither the world, the flesh, nor the devil, is an unspeakably wonderful grace. To achieve this liberation to the full, we must, so to speak, leave the Egypt of sensory satisfaction and cross the desert of spiritual deprivation. When the house of willful appetites is stilled through the mortification of sensuality, the soul is free to walk in genuine authenticity, enjoying union with the Beloved. Renunciation is but a step on the way to lasting liberation.

2

Faith in Darkness

The Active Night of the Spirit
(Book Two, Chapters 1 to 6 of the *Ascent*)

In darkness and secure,
By the secret ladder, disguised,
— Ah, the sheer grace! —
In darkness and concealment,
My house being now all stilled . . .

Faith, according to St. John of the Cross — not works, not ecstatic experiences, only faith — is the proximate means of ascent to union with God. Not only must we let go of sensory gratifications for the sake of going through them to God; we must also relinquish spiritual possessions, like thoughts, dreams, and expectations, and learn to lean on pure faith alone.

The Faces of Faith

Through the use of metaphors and renditions of personal experience, St. John has come to see that faith is, first of all, a "secret ladder." Its "rungs" are hidden from the senses (we believe, though we do not see) and from the spirit (we live, though we do not always know why or for what). Faith is the ladder that leads us to the vantage point from whence we can behold, through a glass darkly, the deep things of God.

Faith is "disguised." That is to say, through faith our sensible and reasonable faculties are changed from what is merely natural to what is spiritual. Donning the disguise of faith, we are able to continue our journey to God, neither recognized nor detained by the world, the flesh, or the devil. These "enemies," says the saint, cannot harm us as long as we walk in the cloak of faith.

On the transcendent level of the spirit, faith redirects the impulses of our vital bodies and the anxieties and ambitions of our functional egos. It puts to rest not only the sensory but also the rational part of the soul. Once this pacification is achieved, the soul "will be joined with the Beloved in a union of simplicity and purity and love and likeness" (*AMC*, II, 1 [2]).

Faith enables the soul to depart in darkness for the land of likeness. It removes impediments in the senses and in the intellect that hold us back. Faith makes us feel secure because the less we rely on our own abilities, the more we can proceed with confidence. It is, therefore, the most admirable means for advancing to God.

Why does St. John compare faith to "midnight" rather than to "twilight" or "dawn"? Faith, he says, is an "obscure habit" that brings one to a belief in divinely revealed truths, which transcend every natural light and infinitely exceed all human understanding. The light of faith in its abundance, like the light of the sun, both dazzles and darkens, suppresses and overwhelms, the light of the human intellect. What it offers as its object is simply too much for the intellect with its logical powers to comprehend. The intellect can master perceived knowledge — as a person can solve an equation — but only through faith does it have the potential to rise to supernatural insight in accordance with the revelations of holy scripture.

Faith, so to speak, subdues the "inferior" intellect so that it can inform the "superior" intellect of matters one has neither the ability to see nor hear, witness or know. Nothing equivalent to God's essential mystery exists in our repertoire of data or information. A premise of faith (for example, belief in the Holy Trinity) is unproportioned to any of our senses. Yet we can know Father, Son, and Holy Spirit as our Creator, Redeemer, and Lover through hearing and believing what faith teaches. Hence, "faith is not a knowledge derived from the senses, but an assent of the soul to what enters through hearing" (*AMC*, II, 3 [3]).

While other knowledge may be acquired by the intellect, it cannot bestow the knowledge given by faith. One who does not believe will not understand (cf. Is 7:9). In short, faith is a "dark night" for us, but, paradoxically, it gives light. "The more darkness it brings . . . the more light it sheds." St. John compares faith to the cloud that separated the children of Israel from the Egyptians. Though dark in itself, it could illumine the night. As it was for them, so must it be for us. Darkness is inescapable on this path if we hope to see the light.

Faith Alone Is Our Guide

It is clear from St. John's reflections that advancing toward union does not depend on understanding, on the support of our own experience, or on feeling, imagination, or memory. Not only must we live in formative detachment or sensory deprivation in regard to temporal things to attain supernatural transformation; we must also be able to suspend rational categories or any pretense to master the mystery. In short, we must lean on dark faith alone as our light and guide.

> Since this transformation and union is something that falls beyond the reach of the senses and of human capability, the soul must empty itself perfectly and

voluntarily — I mean in its affection and will — of all
the earthly and heavenly things it can grasp. It must
through its own efforts empty itself insofar as it can.
As for God, who will stop Him from accomplishing
His desires in the soul that is resigned, annihilated,
and despoiled? (*AMC*, II, 4 [2])

Union with God depends, therefore, on naked belief,
not on anything that can be grasped by desire, imagination, intellect, or any other sense, not on anything known
by means of human ingenuity or experience. This is truly
the *via negativa*. It suggests that the most we can feel and
taste of God in this life is infinitely distant from him. It
requires that we pass beyond everything comprehensible
to the incomprehensible. As St. John puts it: "However
impressive may be one's knowledge or feeling of God,
that knowledge or feeling will have no resemblance to
God and amount to very little."

In explaining what he means by "union with God,"
St. John makes a crucial distinction between substantial
union and union of likeness. He avoids any accusations
of pantheism (in which everything is God) by suggest-
ing that God and the soul become one in participant
transformation (*panentheism*, everything in God but not
identical to God). Only when everything unlike and un-
conformed to God is in the process of being reformed
can the soul recover, so to speak, its lost likeness to God,
that is, can it be through grace "transformed in God."

True, God's sustaining presence never leaves us. This
is his gift of love never to be removed. God's graced
and gracious self-communication to the soul, however,
is bestowed with greater or lesser degrees of intensity
when God so decrees. The initiative for transformation
belongs solely to God. The more one is advanced in love
and conformed to God's will, therefore, the more likely
one is to receive this depth of communication. Hence,
"A person who has reached complete conformity and

likeness of will has attained total supernatural union and transformation in God" (*AMC*, II, 5 [4]).

By contrast, the more one is attached to creatures and weighed down by intellectual pride, the less disposed one is for union. One may not afford God the opportunity (for we humans are free to resist his beckoning or refuse his call) "to transform the soul into the supernatural." What is in reality an immensely complex process of formation, reformation, and transformation is condensed by St. John into one sentence:

> As a result, a man has nothing more to do than strip his soul of these natural contrarieties and dissimilarities so that God who is naturally communicating Himself to it through nature may do so supernaturally through grace (*AMC*, II, 5 [4]).

John then compares this participative union to what happens when a ray of sunlight shines through a smudgy window. Until the smudges are wiped away, the light cannot illumine the window so completely as to transform it into its own shining. The extent of illumination is, of course, not dependent upon the ray of sunlight; it shines no matter what. It is dependent upon the window. The cleaner and purer it is, the more the sunlight will illumine it. Though the two may at the cleanest point seem identical, there will always be a difference between window and ray. Still one can see "that the window is the ray or light of the sun by participation." Consequently, we come to St. John's main point, which bears repeating:

> A man makes room for God by wiping away all the smudges and smears of creatures, by uniting his will perfectly to God's; for to love is to labor to divest and deprive oneself for God of all that is not God. When this is done the soul will be illumined by and transformed in God. And God will so communicate His

supernatural being to it that it will appear to be God Himself and will possess all that God Himself has.

When God grants this supernatural favor to the soul, so great a union is caused that all the things of God and the soul become one in participant transformation, and the soul appears to be God more than a soul. Indeed, it is God by participation. Yet truly, its being (even though transformed) is naturally as distinct from God's as it was before, just as the window, although illumined by the ray, has an existence distinct from the ray (*AMC*, II, 5 [7]).

Preparation for this union requires above all purity and love, much more so than feeling or understanding. The intellect, along with the memory and will, must be cleansed so that we can proceed — in the degree of intensity God allows — to God alone. What hinders us from enjoying this peace and joy "is that one has not attained in his [her] faculties the emptiness required for simple union."

The Way of Faith

The way is at once simple and complex (cf. *AMC*, II, 6 [1]). The way is simple, for "in order to journey to God the intellect must be perfected in the darkness of faith, the memory in the emptiness of hope, and the will in the nakedness and absence of every affection" (understood as any love that becomes a substitute for the love of God). The way is complex, because pride perverts faith by duping us into thinking we can master the Mystery as we might a mathematical problem; possessiveness perverts hope by creating the illusion that we will be fulfilled only if our pre-planned expectations are met; pleasure perverts love by binding enjoyment to temporal delights with no orientation to the transcendent. This perversion is tragic, for it is only via faith, hope, and love that we can be united with God in this life.

Only when faith darkens egocentric understanding
can one advance toward God in hope and love. As faith
obscures what human intellect can grasp, it readies the
soul for divine communications. As hope empties the
memory of past hurts, disappointments, and failures as
well as future plans, projects, and expectations, it readies
the seeker to receive that which is not yet possessed. As
charity deprives one of inordinate affection for all that is
not God or of God, it encourages a leap of love toward
the Trinity with one mind, with one heart.

This shift from ego- to other-centeredness enables us
to follow the lead of grace by emptying our spiritual
faculties of all that is not God for the sake of God. By
the method St. John proposes, these three central formation powers (intellect, memory, and will) can abide
in the "house" of the three foundational dispositions
(faith, hope, and love), for these alone are the proximate means to and the preparation of the soul for union
with God.

It is good for us to know that this method provides
"complete security against the cunning of the devil and
the power of self-love in all its ramifications" (AMC, II,
6 [7]). Wise spiritual master that he is, St. John knows
that it is usually self-love that deceives and hinders our
journey. Hence, by means of these three movements of
believing, hoping, and loving, we learn how to temper
the blind tendency to draw everything down to the level
of ego-gratification. By so doing, we begin to find our
way to the substance and purity of spiritual good, to
God who is, was, and will be.

The gate is Christ. He is the beginning and the end
of our journey. To go to him, we must let go of all sensible and temporal attachments that have become God-
substitutes. In short, we must love God more than *all
of them*. Such is the task of the night of the senses, to
collapse the deception that sense objects can be sources

of ultimate fulfillment. It follows that passing onto this straight path also involves the removal of obstacles related to the spiritual part of the soul.

St. John thus sees a double meaning emerging from Matthew 7:14. The "narrow gate" applies to the sensitive or emotional dimension and the "straight way" to the spiritual or rational part of the soul. To climb the mount of conformity to Christ, we must travel lightly. To seek and gain God, we must soar free. We must run, not walk, through the narrow gate and onto the straight path. To pass over into the sensitive realm, we need wings of selflessness; to pass over into the spiritual realm, we need wings of humility and poverty of spirit. For St. John it is and remains a puzzle that so few travel a road that has been made understandable, practical, and attractive by none other than God's own Son, the second person of the Trinity, who is Emmanuel, God-with-us.

3

To Lose Is to Gain

The Journey in Faith
(Book Two, Chapters 7 to 11 of the *Ascent*)

If anyone wants to be a follower of mine, let him renounce himself and take up his cross and follow me.
Anyone who wants to save his life will lose it; but
anyone who loses his life for my sake, and for the
sake of the gospel, will save it (Mk 8:34–35).

The mystery of loss for the sake of gain is the keynote
of this section of the *Ascent*. St. John knew from personal
experience what it was like to be betrayed, humiliated,
scorned, and forgotten as was Christ in the Garden of
Gethsemane, on the Mount of Calvary. Yet St. John's
faith, like Christ's, never faltered. He knew there was
much to be gained in apparent loss.

The paradox of the paschal mystery, where from
death's door new life springs forth, is ample evidence
for him that there is more to suffering than meets the
eye. To grow in faith is thus not a matter of performing
ascetical feats but of attaining poverty of spirit. Adding
pious activities to the rest of what we do is useless if
we do not acknowledge that there is nothing we can do
without God.

Spiritual mediocrity, by contrast, is content with a degree of virtue. One sets a time and place for prayer but

lacks passion. A few disciplines and mortifications are acquired but one never achieves "the nakedness, poverty, selflessness, or spiritual purity (which are all the same) that the Lord counsels us here" (*AMC*, II, 7 [5]). One clings to spiritual feelings and consolations and would be hard pressed to let these go for God's sake.

The first major test of faith occurs when we are able to distinguish between the consolations of God and the God who consoles. Outer self-denial is insufficient for faith if we are inwardly encapsulated by spiritual pride — proud of our holiness while missing the entire point of imitating Christ's poverty of spirit.

St. Francis of Assisi's description of "perfect joy" is comparable to what St. John of the Cross calls "perfect food." Francis tells Brother Leo, much to his amazement, that true joy is not to be found in the news that all the masters of theology in Paris have joined the order along with all the archbishops, bishops, and kings of France and England, nor that his friars have gone to the unbelievers and converted all of them to the faith nor that he himself can heal the sick or perform miracles. He explains what Christian joy is by telling a story:

I am returning from Perugia and I am coming here at night, in the dark. It is winter time and wet and muddy and so cold that icicles form at the edges of my habit and keep striking my legs, and blood flows from such wounds. And I come to the gate, all covered with mud and cold and ice, and after I have knocked and called for a long time, a friar comes and asks: "Who are you?" I answer: "Brother Francis." And he says: "Go away. This is not a decent time to be going about. You can't come in."

And when I insist again, he replies: "Go away. You are a simple and uneducated fellow. From now on don't stay with us any more. We are so many and so important that we don't need you."

But I still stand at the gate and say: "For the love
of God, let me come in tonight." And he answers: "I
won't. Go to the Crosiers' Place and ask there."
    I tell you that if I kept patience and was not upset —
that is true joy and true virtue and the salvation of the
soul (St. Francis of Assisi, *Omnibus of Sources* [Chicago:
Franciscan Herald Press, 1972], pp. 1501–02).

Accepting the Cross

Both saints knew the danger of having what St. John
calls a "spiritual sweet tooth." How many, when offered the solid food of the cross (dryness, distaste, trial),
"run from it as from death and wander about in search
only of sweetness and delightful communications from
God. Such an attitude is not the hallmark of self-denial
and nakedness of spirit, but the indication of a 'spiritual
sweet tooth' " (*AMC*, II, 7 [5]).

What, then, does being Christ's faithful friend entail? We must realize from the start the stark reality
of *nada*. There is no short cut to Easter morning. One
either drinks from the chalice or passes it by. To take
the cup of suffering in faith is to choose the distasteful,
not the delectable — to be content with desolation until
God sends consolation, to accept dryness and affliction
in joyful abandonment to the Mystery, even when there
is no relief in sight. In brief, it is to deny oneself and
take up the cross. Greater love than this is unimaginable. As Christ emptied the cup so must we; as his will
was united wholly with the Father's so must ours be.
No progress is possible without this kind of spiritual
death. Only by undergoing it can we reclaim, with, in,
and through Christ, life in its abundance. Only when we
accept the cross as our "supporting staff" can we greatly
lighten and ease our load.

We know from St. John's biography that what he says
is true. At his darkest hour, when he was imprisoned

and tortured by his own confreres in Toledo, he composed on scraps of paper and confined to memory poetry so deep that it would later require pages of commentary to unravel only a few layers of meaning. He is his own witness to the fact that "If a man resolutely submits to the carrying of this cross, if he decidedly wants to find and endure trials in all things for God, he will discover in all of them great relief and sweetness" (*AMC*, II, 7 [7]).

The first step to freedom of spirit, as St. John sees it, is utter renunciation of self-centeredness in both the sensible and the spiritual realms. Meditations, methods and manners of prayer may be of help in the beginning of the spiritual life, but they can become obstacles because the longer we live the more we realize that grace, not works, does the leading. The "one thing necessary" is "true self-denial, exterior and interior, through surrender of self both to suffering for Christ and to annihilation in all things. In the exercise of this self-denial everything else, and even more, is discovered and accomplished" (*AMC*, II, 7 [8]).

Thus for St. John self-denial or true humility is the "root and sum total of all the virtues." All other methods end up being counterproductive to progress in the life of the spirit. They may result "in considerations and communications as lofty as those of the angels," but one has not moved an inch along the narrow path. One has missed the entire point that progress is made only through the imitation of Christ, who is the way, the truth, and the life. No one goes to the Father save through him (cf. Jn 14:6). A spirituality that would walk "in sweetness and ease and run from the imitation of Christ" is laughable to St. John.

Conformity to Christ

The death of Jesus that we are to imitate is both sensory and spiritual. The two are intertwined. When Christ felt himself at the extreme point of abandonment, when he experienced himself forsaken by the Father, he accomplished spiritually the most marvelous work of his life, the work of redemption surpassing any miracle he had ever performed on earth.

> He brought about the reconciliation and union of the human race with God through grace. The Lord achieved this . . . at the moment in which He was most annihilated in all things: in His reputation before men, since in beholding Him die they mocked Him instead of esteeming Him; in His human nature, by dying; and in spiritual help and consolation from His Father, for He was forsaken by His Father at that time so as to pay the debt fully and bring man to union with God (*AMC*, II, 7 [11]).

The avenue to union thus entails the annihilation, sensitively and spiritually speaking, of the very ego-self it takes us years to attain. We need not fear, however, that this process will destroy our vitality or render bland our personality. Saints like Francis and John retain distinct temperaments while becoming transparent to Christ. Christ is at the core of their being; he is their heart of hearts; it is no longer they who live but Christ who lives through them. What the saints esteem are not their own comforts or talents, admirable as these may be, but the deepest selves they are called to be in Christ. By allowing him to bring them to "nothing," they become "everything" he wants them to be.

This journey, therefore, "does not consist in recreations, experiences, and spiritual feelings, but in the living, sensory and spiritual, exterior and interior death of the cross" (*AMC*, II, 7 [11]). To say one is a friend of Christ and to remain imprisoned by self-love and the seeking of personal consolations is a gross deception. Extensive learning, high repute, worldly pretensions and rank can potentially hinder our knowing Christ and block the freedom that comes with faith. Saddest is the case of persons whom God has called to the banquet but who refuse to come because their intellects, their powers of rationalization, get in the way of faith; their memories block hope; their wills choose other "gods." Thus St. John's first obligation is to show that only faith — not anything created, imagined, or intellectually known — can serve as the true and proper means for union with God.

Purification of the Intellect

Because the human mind with its bent toward *hubris* can distort the truth and lead souls astray, St. John feels obliged to devote the bulk of the *Ascent* to an analysis of how and why the intellect must be purified by faith. His initial argument is as follows. While creatures carry a trace of God, God as he is in himself bears no essential likeness to them. In fact, everything the finite intellect can understand, the will experience, or the imagination picture is most unlike and disproportionate to God's infinite being. Hence if mind and heart are to draw near to God, it is necessary that one advance more by unknowing than by knowing. This is because "the intellect will not be able through its ideas to understand anything like God, nor the will experience a delight and sweetness resembling Him, or the memory place in the fantasy remembrances and images representing Him" (*AMC*, II, 8 [5]).

Mystical theology, contemplation, the secret wisdom of God — these terms become almost synonymous in St. John's vocabulary. In this he is faithful to one of his oft-quoted teachers, Pseudo-Dionysius who, in *The Mystical Theology*, insists that to know God is in fact not to know God. Paradoxically "the brightest light in God is complete darkness to our intellect" (*AMC*, II, 8 [6]).

Does this mean that if one longs to be united with
God one must vow to become an anti-intellectual? Were
this the case St. John himself would have to be disqual-
ified as a candidate for the grace of union because he
was unquestionably a brilliant spiritual theologian. The
intellect is not the problem; arrogance is. Hence, pride
of mind can be tamed only in the midnight of faith.

Faith is the only proximate and proportionate means
by which the human mind can grasp and enjoy union
with God. To prepare for this union, grace like a consuming fire has, where God is concerned, to cleanse and
empty the intellect of everything related to sensate apprehension. Faith alone can lead the way. For the likeness between faith and God is so close that "no other
difference exists than that between believing in God and
seeing Him" (AMC, II, 9 [1]).

Faith leads us to a kind of second innocence in which
the mind, purified and silenced, can at last open itself
in childlike confidence to the wonder of God, whose
essence rises above understanding, who appears to us
as fire by day and cloud by night. When mortal life itself
is shattered by death, faith remains to carry us on wings
of dawn to "the glory and light of the divinity."

Knowledge in the Intellect

In brief, the intellect is seen by St. John as the recipient of two main types of knowledge: natural and supernatural. Natural knowledge is in effect the product
of what we understand by means of the bodily senses
and through reflection. Supernatural knowledge refers to
everything imparted to the intellect in a way that transcends its natural ability and capacity.

There are in turn two kinds of supernatural knowledge — corporal and spiritual. Both are further
subdivided into two categories. Corporal knowledge

originates from the exterior bodily senses of sight, hearing, smell, taste, and touch and consists also of knowledge received from the interior bodily senses, including all that imagination can apprehend, form, and fashion by means of the fantasy. Spiritual knowledge consists of distinct particular apprehensions communicated to the spirit without means of bodily senses, these being visions, revelations, locutions, and spiritual feelings. Dark general contemplation imparted in faith is the goal toward which the soul will be led by guiding it through these other apprehensions and divesting them of their power to entrap the soul and hinder it from transcending.

To all of these forms of natural and supernatural knowledge, save that of dark general contemplation, St. John will in the end say *nada*. Nothing they can stir up or speculate upon has anything to do with the essential being and mystery of God, which beckons us to deepest intimacy.

The need to purify "corporal spiritual knowledge" is as important today as it was when St. John addressed the topic over four hundred years ago. As human beings, knowledge of things reaches our intellect by means of the five bodily senses St. John refers to as "exterior." The apprehensions received via our senses must be appraised with utmost scrutiny. When supernatural objects are presented to the intellect by means of the senses, they are always subject to distortion. This is why St. John devoted the first book of the *Ascent* to the "night of sense." The active night must be applied not only to ordinary detachment from sensate "idols" but also to the supernatural representations and objects presented to spiritual persons by means of the senses. What might some of these be?

Before answering this question, let us remember that St. John lived in a time, not unlike our own, when people were undergoing awakening experiences in authentic and pseudo-spiritual ways. Luminaries, flagellants, sorcerers, and seers were as prevalent as genuine mystics like himself and St. Teresa of Avila. In this highly charged atmosphere, both saints were firm in their warnings that the more "corporeal" visions, locutions, and similar extraordinary phenomenon were, the less they could be trusted. Even if they were beheld by truly spiritual persons, only too familiar with the need for detachment from such apprehensions, they were still to be distrusted. We must never rely on them or accept them. We must flee completely from them. We must have no desire to determine if they are good or bad. These include spiritual apprehensions that come: from *sight*, such as visions of the dead, as a seance might produce, or seeings of saints, of good and bad angels, of unusual lights and splendors as, for example, piercing sunrays or auras; from *hearing*, such as extraordinary words uttered by visionary or envisioned persons or coming from unknown sources or from the oft-quoted "Holy Spirit who told me . . ."; from *smell*, such as sweet fragrances (the "odor of sanctity") that have no known origin; from *taste*, such as "exquisite savors"; and from *touch* or "spiritual unction" or the sensation of "extreme delight," such as spine-tingling affections in which one is inclined almost to swoon with pleasure, feelings so intense "that all the bones and marrow rejoice, flourish, and bathe in [them]" (*AMC*, II, 11 [1]).

Corporeal Cautions

The essence of St. John's critique is this: The more exterior and corporeal these feelings and sensations are, the less sure one can be of their divine origin. Who is

to say, especially in a group setting, where psychic con-
tagion leaves off and genuine inspiration begins? How
many qualified spiritual directors are available to help
the faithful engage in such a profound discernment process? Clearly the mind, stimulated by highly charged
intentions toward attaining holiness and by volatile sensual experiences, can interpret as God-given what is
merely of human origin. St. John says it is wise, if anything, to consider such manifestations more diabolical
than divine. In the realm of sense perception of spiritual
apprehensions, there is much danger and much room for
deception. One can easily mistake the forest for the trees.
One can start to feel quite special, holier-than-thou, and
still remain ignorant of spiritual matters.

Why is attentiveness to these exteriorly received spiritual communications so dangerous and such a hindrance
to progress? Besides being an occasion for error, presumption, and vanity, such apprehensions of the transcendent may tempt a person to forsake faith and
instead to follow after these communications in the belief
that their light, their fascination, their sheer extraordi-
nariness, is the guide and means to union with God. Yet
as has been made clear over and over again by St. John,
faith alone is the way to oneness.

Any form of spiritual pride is, of course, contrary to
humility. The so-called "privileged one," the recipient of
"special favors," may secretly slip into developing a fine
opinion of him- or herself, a hidden self-satisfaction on
which the devil will play. For this reason St. John holds
that such representations and feelings must always be
rejected. Otherwise no progress through the dark nights
of sense and spirit is possible.

When and if a vision, affection or locution is authen-
tically of God, it produces an edifying effect in the spirit
"at the very moment of its perception, without allowing any deliberation about wanting or not wanting it"

(*AMC*, II, 11 [6]). Here the initiative belongs to God. He grants these favors without the help of our ability or efforts. He gives the gift or withholds it. We are merely recipients not purveyors. God produces the effect he desires passively in the deepest part of the soul. What he does, does not depend on our wanting or not wanting the communication.

To clarify this point, St. John draws the following analogy:

> Were fire to come into immediate contact with a person's flesh, that person's desire not to be burned would hardly be helpful, for the fire will produce its effect necessarily. So too with good visions and sensible communications: Even when a person dismisses them, they produce their effect first and foremost in the soul rather than in the body (*AMC*, II, 11 [6]).

Harms Incurred by Attending to Sensory Communications

The effects of "diabolical" as opposed to "divine" communications are, among others, agitation, dryness, vanity, or presumption — all more harmful to spiritual progress than efficacious. They cause unrest, lack of courage, and circumspection. How different are God's self-communications, which penetrate the soul like fragrant oil softens dry, cracked skin. They move the will to love. They leave their effect imprinted on our hearts forever. Even if one wants to resist such divine onslaughts, one cannot — no more than a "window can withstand the sunlight shining on it," to use one of the saint's favorite analogies.

In summary, St. John lists six kinds of harm that can occur if we make the mistake of accepting these communications as proximate means to union, even if their origin is divine. Even to the most authentic communication of this sort, one must in the end say *nada*, not to its efficacious effects, but to the corporal articulation or interpretation of them.

The harms St. John sees as obvious are these:

1. *A diminishment of faith.* It is simply true that sensible experiences detract from faith. They incline a person to seek proof, to want guarantees, to fall back, and fail to persevere without felt consolations.

2. *A lessening of transcendence.* This happens because sensible experiences, due to their vital residues, can prevent the mind from moving beyond the visible to the invisible, or from moving through the finite epiphanies of the Mystery to the Mystery itself in all its fullness.

3. *A possessive attitude.* One can go so far as to "collect" divine communications, to seek "spiritual highs," to maneuver from one mountaintop experience to another while never settling into the valley of fidelity where the journey to God includes "genuine renunciation and nakedness of spirit."

4. *Loss of efficaciousness.* Exactly because one sets his or her eyes on the sensible aspect of spiritual apprehensions, one is likely to miss the interior spirituality they are intended to produce. It is as if one mistakes the means for the end or assumes that a puddle is the ocean itself.

5. *Loss of God's favors.* Insofar as we tend to receive these gifts as if they belong to us, as if we merit or deserve them, we cannot profit from them. Before long we are inclined to think that these favors are self-initiated rather than wholly God-generated.

6. *Openness to diabolical temptation.* Taken in total, these harms obviously make one more than ever prone to demonic seduction or manipulation. The prince of darkness can transform himself into an angel of light (cf. 2 Cor 11:14). So dangerous is this terrain that St. John

again advises the faithful to reject these apprehensions
with closed eyes. Once the devil slips in, diabolical representations will multiply and divine communication will
gradually cease — so much so that eventually "all will
come from the devil and none at all from God." Incau-
tious people, lacking in spiritual wisdom, may grow so
dependent on these communications that they will have
a difficult time, to say the least, in returning to God
through purity of faith.

Sound Advice

A step in the right direction is paradoxically to close
oneself off inwardly, to radically detach oneself from
good or bad spiritual apprehensions. If good, their effects will show up anyway; if bad, they will be elimi-
nated from the start.

God customarily grants favors to humble, dispossessed persons, who live by faith and do not attend
much, if at all, to supernatural favors clung to with the
senses. The more one lets go of sense-satisfying morsels,
the more God will bestow a higher quality of food. In
short, St. John advises us not to clutch onto sensory communications. Do not be encumbered by them, for "The
fly that clings to honey hinders its flight, and the soul
that allows its attachment to spiritual sweetness hinders
its own liberty and contemplation" (*Sayings of Light and
Love*, No. 24).

Neither visions nor any other form of sense apprehension can serve as a means toward union, for they bear
no proportion to God. It is as if St. John is saying that
to desire consolations or divine communications is to
expose oneself wittingly or unwittingly to temptation —
and why take a chance? Why not simply wait upon God
and allow God to take the initiative where transformation of heart is concerned? Why not trust that "The very

pure spirit does not meddle with exterior attachments or human respect, but it communes inwardly with God, alone and in solitude as to all forms, and with delightful tranquillity, for the knowledge of God is received in divine silence" (*Sayings of Light and Love*, No. 26)?

4

Touched by the Transcendent

The Call to Contemplation

(Book Two, Chapters 12 to 15 of the *Ascent*)

In a world dependent on mass media to spark its imagination, in a culture attached to audiovisual aids for sensual stimulation, St. John of the Cross boldly proposes deprivation as a positive good. Natural imaginative apprehensions, however blissful, he says, are inadequate means for attaining union with God. They are, if anything, harmful impediments. The saint's conclusions shock the senses. To read the *Ascent*, as I have often said, is like taking a cold shower in a frosty apartment on a snowy morning when the furnace is shut off. In his calm, methodical fashion, the saint invites us to think twice about what constitutes real, as opposed to imaginative, contemplation.

A Divesting Process

The movement to contemplation is neither a matter of exterior stimulation nor of satiating the imagination with interior phantasies. The opposite must occur. A process of "denuding" or "divesting" sensate powers of their natural apprehensions and appetites through the active "night of sense" is essential. The same divesting must be applied to supernatural apprehensions received imaginatively through the corporeal senses as grace guides us into the active "night of the spirit."

To prepare us to follow and flow with the call to contemplation, St. John must first identify the impediments to spiritual progress associated with the imagination and the phantasy, both of which are fed by corporal or sensual stimuli. In the childhood of the spiritual life, the use of images and concepts as food for meditation is invaluable. Roman Catholic children learn about their faith from seeing pictures in the Bible, from hearing the church choir, smelling incense, lighting candles, touching the crucifix, participating in a May crowning. Later they may be instructed to use their imagination to meditate on scenes from the life of Jesus or to picture in detail the mysteries of the Rosary or the Stations of the Cross. The trouble is that many mistake these imaginative meditations as proximate means to union with God. Actually both the imagination and the phantasy must be "darkened" if one is to reach divine union. The question is: When do these faculties cease to be servant sources of contemplation? Why must they be superseded by another movement?

A handy formula to remember might be: Imagination as a discursive power (moving our interior mind narratively, as it were, from point to point) plus phantasy as an image-forming power (feeding the narrative capacity of the imagination) equals meditation, defined by St. John as "a discursive act built upon forms, figures, and images, imagined and fashioned by these senses" (*AMC*, II, 12 [3]). An example might be dwelling upon some scene from the life of Jesus like the wedding feast of Cana (Jn 2:1–11) or reflecting line by line upon a text from the psalms, gospels or Paulinian epistles.

Where natural imaginative apprehensions are concerned, St. John concludes: "The soul will have to empty itself of these images and leave this sense in darkness if it is to reach divine union" (*AMC*, II, 12 [3]). None of these material images and figures, in other words, no manifestations of the Mystery, can in and of themselves be an adequate means toward union with God. On this point, St. John will not compromise. He believes firmly, as does St. Paul, that "eye has not seen, ear has not heard . . . what God has prepared for those who love him" (cf. 1 Cor 2:9).

Images like a rose, a sea, a stained glass window, presented to the imagination through the exterior senses, *cannot* be either a proper or a proximate means to union with God in the fullness of his glory. The soul has to empty itself of these images and follow the lead of grace, which draws also interior imaginative senses into the darkness of faith.

Natural imagination, stimulated and discursively applied, is an important faculty for meditation. It is not adequate for the work of "secret" contemplation, however. Dependent as this faculty is on external stimuli (what eyes have seen, what ears have heard), it can at most compose *resemblances* of what has been beheld or touched or tasted. But what are resemblances compared to the real thing? What is any limping trace of the mystery compared to divine Love itself? What is an imaginary palace of pearl or a mountain of gold compared to one real bead, one gleaming nugget? The imagination can picture this or that reality, but no picture can capture and hold the elusive rainbow of reality. Similarly, to follow St. John's reasoning, just as created things are by virtue of their creation unproportioned to the uncreated majesty of God, so "all imaginings fashioned out of their similarities are incapable of serving as proximate means toward union with Him" (*AMC*, II, 12 [4]).

Means, Not Ends

What the saint teaches here is vital if we are to maintain and strengthen our faith. How many avowedly reject God or profess atheism on the basis of an image they hold of God? Often the God they deny or say they do not know is a God fashioned out of their own or others' imagination. Many, for example, despise God as "father" because they project onto the divine mystery an image of their human fathers, who were perhaps abusive, stern, unforgiving, relentlessly punishing, or slyly seductive. As some theologians would say, the "god" they have killed had to die so the God beyond all images could reveal himself to them once again. Those who imagine God under the guise of any humanly fashioned figure, be it fire or light, are, in St. John's words, "very far from Him."

It is fair to say, however, that considerations, forms, images, methods, and techniques that aid meditation are and remain helpful to beginners on the path to deeper prayer. God uses these means to "woo" the soul to himself, to set the stage for spiritual awakening. In this sense St. John refers to them as "remote means" (vs. proximate) to attain union with God. They pave the road for, but do not in themselves grant, spiritual repose. The danger is that the spiritually awakened person may mistake a signpost for the destination, resting in these means and ceasing to advance to the goal who is the "Supreme Repose and Good in this life" (*AMC*, II, 12 [5]).

What happens to people who do not know how to detach themselves from palpable methods? How can a good spiritual director help them? Here St. John asks in effect another question. What is God's intent in drawing awakened souls beyond images and meditative techniques? His answer is clear and direct: "God . . . wishes to lead them to more spiritual, interior, and invisible

graces by removing the gratification derived from discursive meditation" (AMC, II, 12 [6]). The way up, in
other words, is the way down — down to deeper foun-
dations of faith where one learns to cling to the God
who consoles rather than holding on to used clothing
(these methods) as if it had to be a permanent part of
one's wardrobe.

The opposite scenario finds the well-meaning but
mistaken beginner striving hard to meditate, perhaps
frowning in concentration or cocking an ear to hear
the slightest cymbal clash of consolation. Despite every
effort, one finds only more aridity, fatigue, and rest-
lessness of soul. Do eager beginners get the message?
Hardly. The more arid the desert, the harder they strain
toward a drink, only to discover that their desired oasis
is an elusive mirage.

It is as if God sets before us a dish of gourmet deli-
cacies beautifully prepared but instead of enjoying it we
rush out the door to purchase the ingredients. The food
God wants to give us is "delicate, interior, and spiritual."
The source of this nourishment is not the labor of our
imagination but God's gift. Our place is not to work for
it but to remain in peace, in quiet, in repose — to remain,
in other words, ready and receptive to the movements
of the Spirit by one general and pure act of love rather
than hammering out particular acts with our imaginative or willful faculties. God's work in us will take the
lead. All we have to do is follow. Remember: "If everything consisted of going, one would never arrive; and
if everywhere we found means, when and where could
one enjoy the end and goal?" (AMC, II, 12 [6]).

The tug of war between grace and our own efforts
to control its pace understandably causes us to lose the
peace God wants to grant us. Grace desires that the one
who prays learns to abide in the "calm and repose of

interior quietude," refreshed at the wellspring of heavenly love. The pray-er, not heeding the signals that some deeper waters are being stirred, goes backward to cling stubbornly to exterior considerations that repel the soul that "would want to remain in that unintelligible peace as its right place" (*AMC*, II, 12 [7]).

How strange all this is: God is granting rest — what we really want — but we persist in going back to work, perhaps because that is what makes us feel as if we are in control. The whole situation is ludicrous. It would be as if an elegant person invited us to Sunday brunch on a day when we had nothing better to do, but we refused the invitation and said we preferred to scrub the kitchen floor, remake the beds, hoe the garden, and go to bed hungry!

From the point of view of God's initiative at this stage of prayer, St. John insists rather emphatically that we can do nothing. The more we try of our own efforts to attain satisfaction, the more aridity we feel. Paradoxically, the more intense our efforts are, the less is our gain. The more we persist in acts of discursive meditation, the further we drag ourselves away from spiritual peace. In fact, says the saint, we resemble fools who abandon great treasure for trite goods, who turn back on a road already traversed, who redo a task that has already been done.

Signs of Passing on to Contemplation

What, then, does the master advise as the proper response to these graced outpourings drawing us to a state of contemplation? What he counsels can be expressed in a series of small imperatives, namely:

1. Learn to abide in quietude with loving attentiveness to God (this will certainly temper your ego-control).

2. Pay no heed to the imagination and its work (this will certainly diminish your distractions).

3. Let your faculties (intellect, memory, will) remain in a state of rest.

4. Passively receive divine direction rather than actively doing something (this allows you to remain receptive to what God is effecting in you).

5. If you must put your faculties to work, do not make use of excessive efforts or studied reasonings.

6. Whatever you do, do so with the gentleness of love, moved more by God than by your own abilities.

These suggestions are offered to anyone who wants to aspire toward advancement in the life of the spirit. St. John trusts by now that we understand how suitable and necessary it is to detach ourselves from methods, ways, and uses of the imagination and follow docilely the lead of grace. Spiritual directors and directees must recognize the "signs" by which to verify the interior movements of the Spirit, inviting one to discontinue reasoning and imagining and to dwell with God in loving attentiveness. How do we know if we should cease discursive meditation for a while and pass on to the Spirit-initiated state of contemplation? When is the opportune time to do so, considering the fact that imaginative apprehensions, while not a proximate means toward union for proficients, are a remote means for beginners?

The signs a discerning heart needs to observe are these three:

1. "The realization that one cannot make discursive meditation nor receive satisfaction from it as before" (*AMC*, II, 13 [2]). Let's say you felt stirred to adore God by picturing in your mind's eye the gospel scene where Jesus blesses the children (cf. Lk 18:15–17). Dwelling on it you sensed how good it was to trust Providence, to recognize and repent for the times you refused to turn your life over to God. As long as you derive satisfaction

from such a meditation, St. John cautions: Do not abandon it. Whereas once it bestowed a certain delight, now dryness is the outcome. Still it is not wise to let go of this method until grace draws you into the peace and quietude associated with the "third sign."

2. "An awareness of a disinclination to fix the imagination or sense faculties on particular objects, exterior or interior" (*AMC*, II, 13 [3]). Let us say you could be assured of deeper reverence by imagining a crucifix or by remembering your sense of God's nearness following the singing of a beautiful hymn. Whereas you used to be inclined spontaneously to devote your mind and heart to God in these particular acts, now you are disinclined to do so. Certainly images come and go (even in deep recollection the imagination wanders freely) but the issue here is a "disinclination" to set your sense faculties or imaginative powers upon extraneous things as such.

3. "The third and surest sign is that a person likes to remain alone in loving awareness of God, without particular considerations, in interior peace and quiet and repose, and without the acts and exercises . . . of the intellect, memory and will" (*AMC*, II, 13 [4]). This bent toward solitude is accompanied by a growing preference not to meditate discursively, that is, by proceeding from point to point as in the early stages of the Ignatian exercises. Preferred is the disposition of waiting upon the Spirit with a general, loving awareness, without any particular knowledge or understanding. It is as if the soul senses in awe: "I look at God, God looks at me."

The Signs at Work Together

St. John cautions that it is safe to pass over the state of meditation into that of contemplation only if one is led by the Spirit and if he or she, along with an experienced spiritual director, observes these three signs at work *to-gether*. Were only the first sign prominent, it could mean that one's inability to meditate imaginatively might be due to mere dissipation of mind and the absence or lack of diligence. The second sign, a disinclination to think about extraneous things, must be present as well. These two signs together, without the third, are also insufficient. The cause of both dissipation and disinclination, in line with the psychological understanding of the time, could be "melancholia . . . capable of producing a certain stupefaction and suspension of the sense faculties" (*AMC*, II, 13 [6]). Today we might speak of the symptom of "low grade depression." As St. John suggests, this condition may lead to extreme mood swings, one day melancholic malaise, the next a longing to soar upward in "delightful ravishment."

Little wonder the saint insists on the presence of the third sign, loving knowledge, and, in fact, on all three appearing together. Such knowledge is at first extremely subtle and delicate, almost imperceptible. It is difficult to appraise its appearance properly, for one has become accustomed to the exercise of discursive meditation, "which is wholly sensible." Thus one "hardly perceives or feels this new insensible, purely spiritual experience" (*AMC*, II, 13 [7]). Yet trusting that it is of the Spirit and flowing with it ensures that the loving knowledge of God will grow and become more evocative of peace, rest, and joy than anything one knew before.

To prove his point, St. John gives two reasons why the first sign (the inability to make discursive meditation) comes about. Obviously when God has granted all the good obtainable from a practice, God will then invite a person to move ahead on the path of prayer. Life, understood spiritually, is an upwardly, always transcending movement. As the saint wrote in the fourth stanza of one of his poems in *The Collected Works*, entitled "More Stanzas Applied to Spiritual Things" :

> In a wonderful way
> My one flight surpassed a thousand,
> For the hope of heaven
> Attains as much as it hopes for;
> This seeking is my only hope
> And I have not been disappointed,
> Because I flew so high, so high
> That I took the prey.

Moving on is possible precisely because one has acquired a substantial and habitual stance of meditation. This discipline is good. One will obviously return to it, but for now, because it no longer bestows spiritual gratification, one can indeed leave behind the particulars of knowledge gained and abide in general loving awareness of "the captured prey" (*AMC*, II, 14 [3]). To settle for "the rind of the spirit" (images, concepts, reasonings) when one is beginning to enjoy "the substance of the fruit" (loving quietude) would not make much sense. At this juncture of the spiritual life, the less we understand the further we may be able to penetrate into the night of the spirit, passing through it to "a union with God beyond all knowing."

Regarding the second sign, it comes about exactly because one feels a longing for what St. John refers to in his poetry as "I-don't-know-what / Which is so gladly found" (see "Commentary Applied to Spiritual Things," Verse 1). In the light of this longing, one necessarily finds all worldly images and reasoning processes utterly dissatisfying.

Still the third sign is a "must" before discontinuing discursive meditation. It reflects the real condition of a person who has left one stage of prayer but has not quite found another. A shift from meditation to contemplation is taking place through the power of the Holy Spirit but, from the point of view of the person, it feels as if one is and can do nothing. One senses being in a state of inactivity but clearly it is better to be there than to move back to an old way or to force a new one. One feels suspended, in other words, "between the drudgery of a journey and the rest and quiet gladdening its end," "between cooking a meal and eating without effort what has already been...prepared" (*AMC*, II, 14 [7]).

First Fruits of Contemplative Knowledge

On the one hand, the sensory faculties that seek out and form knowledge from this or that source of input are idle as to the work of discursive meditation; on the other hand, the spiritual faculties are receiving, often without feeling anything, the first fruits of a general, simple, more perfect contemplative knowing. Paradoxically, the purer this general knowledge is, the darker it seems to the perceiving intellect. St. John's illustration of a window through which sunlight streams is worth quoting in its entirety:

> In observing a ray of sunlight stream through the window, we notice that the more it is pervaded with particles of dust, the clearer and more palpable and sensible it appears to the senses; yet obviously the sun ray in itself is less pure, clear, simple, and perfect in that it is full of so many specks of dust. We also notice that when it is more purified of these specks of dust it seems more obscure and impalpable to the material eye; and the purer it is, the more obscure and inapprehensible it seems to be. If the ray of sunlight should be entirely cleansed and purified of all dust particles, even the most minute, it would appear totally obscure and incomprehensible to the eye, since visible things, the object of the sense of sight, would be absent. Thus the eye would find no images on which to rest, because light is not the proper object

of sight, but only the means through which visible
things are seen. If there is nothing visible off which
the ray of light can reflect, nothing will be seen. If the
ray, then, were to enter through one window and go
out another without striking any quantitative object,
it would be invisible. Yet the ray of sunlight would
be purer and cleaner than when, on account of being filled with visible objects, it is more manifestly
perceived (*AMC*, II, 14 [9]).

Of course, supernatural knowledge is comparable to
the sunlight, natural knowledge to the specks of dust.
The purer the knowledge of contemplation is, the more
invisible it is to the intellect and the more it effects a
noticeable darkness, a kind of oblivion. The "suspension" can be such that you are drawn for hours into
such a state that you do not know what has occurred
or how the time has passed. An hour may seem like
a minute, so lost are you in awe and wonder. However long the prayer of simple union may last, it seems
of brief duration, for oneness with pure knowledge, according to St. John, is independent of time. However
short it is, this prayer pierces the heavens. Yet its effects are unmistakable: "an elevation of mind to heavenly knowledge, and a withdrawal and abstraction from
all objects, forms, and figures as well as from the remembrance of them" (*AMC*, II, 14 [11]). Of his own experience, the saint wrote in Verses 6 and 7 of his poem,
"Stanzas Concerning an Ecstasy Experienced in High
Contemplation":

> This knowledge in unknowing
> Is so overwhelming
> That wise men disputing
> Can never overthrow it,
> For their knowledge does not reach
> To the understanding of not understanding,
> Transcending all knowledge.

> And this supreme knowledge
> Is so exalted
> That no power of man or learning
> Can grasp it;
> He who masters himself
> Will, with knowledge in unknowing,
> Always be transcending.

While the utilitarian-functional mind might label such experiences a "waste of time," St. John has another opinion. Work with the senses, he says, may be idled for now, but on another plane a profound transformation is occurring.

> This communication, consequently, is called a general, loving knowledge, for just as it is imparted obscurely to the intellect, so too a vague delight and love is given to the will without distinct knowledge of the object loved (AMC, II, 14 [12]).

Indeed, the saint adds in the same text, "the higher and more sublime the divine light, the darker it is to our intellect."

One who is a "proficient" in the spiritual life, who has heard the call to contemplation and responded to it, will still at times return to the practice of discursive meditation until grace makes perfect this new "habit." Though you meditate in a familiar manner, you discover more often than not something new. Noticeable at a certain point may be the fact that every time you intend to meditate you are suddenly lifted up, but not by any power of your own. There is in your life of prayer a rhythm of meditation and contemplation, of working gently with your inner faculties to aid adoration and yet of being led by the Spirit into a state of peace and repose where the work of union is being done in your soul without any effort. For what is there to do? Nothing, "besides attentively loving God and refraining from the desire to feel or see anything" (AMC, II,

15 [2]). Light is infused supernaturally into the receptive soul by no other effort than that of receiving what is bestowed. Illumination leads to "obscure knowledge" without the lights of the "forms, concepts, or figures of meditative discourse" (*AMC*, II, 15 [3]). For what are "tangible lights" compared to the "serene, limpid light" of the Spirit?

St. John believes that this light is never lacking. It is God's greatest gift to us, but our fallen condition blocks the entrance of the light into our deepest soul. As we begin to let go of sinful impediments and live in true poverty of spirit, turning always to God as flowers to the sun, we shall soon be transformed into the persons we were meant by God to be.

The final counsel St. John has to offer us can be contained in effect in two words: *Don't worry*. If you cannot meditate for all the reasons given, simply remain in God's presence with loving attention, with a tranquil mind. Even if it seems that you are idle, trust that a deeper stirring is in process. Little by little, you will be enveloped in a divine calm and peace. The wondrous, sublime knowledge of God will be infused into your soul. Don't interfere with what is occurring. Don't clutter your inner room with discursive meditations and imaginings. Wait upon your Divine Guest and let him wait upon you. He prefers an empty room where you alone wait. To paraphrase St. Teresa of Avila, let nothing disturb you, nothing disquiet you, nothing draw you out of your peaceful contentment. This pacification of soul is after all no small accomplishment. It is rather all that the Lord asks of us through the psalmist when he says: "Learn to be empty of all things — interiorly and exteriorly — and you will behold that I am God" (*AMC*, II, 15 [5]).

5

Nothing Only God

The Misleading Power of
Supernatural Phenomena

(Book Two, Chapters 16 to 22 of the *Ascent*)

Since God is inaccessible, be careful not to concern
yourself with all that your faculties can comprehend
and your senses feel, so that you do not become satisfied with less and lose the lightness of soul suitable
for going to Him (*Sayings of Light and Love*, No. 52).

All too often spiritual experience is equated with the
extraordinary, yet over and over again St. John insists
that neither natural nor supernatural apprehensions can
be proximate means to union with God. No vision of any
sort, however edifying, can of itself ever approximate
the divine mystery to which it points. A vision is but
a shadow of the real thing. It may catch our attention
like a flash of lightning, but it would be as unwise to
dwell upon it as it would be to expose ourselves to an
electrical charge.

We must exercise extreme caution in regard to extraordinary phenomena. Like the people of St. John's
time, we, too, live in an era where "spiritual experience" is increasingly sought. Witness the number who
pilgrimage to sites of alleged apparitions, to say nothing of "new age" events. People publish accounts of their

"spiritual highs" in popular journals. Amidst such sound and fury, often signifying nothing, it is wise to heed anew the saint's astute analysis of "visions" and related phenomena.

Defining the "Supernatural"

St. John says that by "imaginative vision" he means "everything supernaturally represented to the imagination under the category of image, form, figure, and species" (*AMC*, II, 16 [2]). Our consciousness is composed in such a way that sights or showings can be impressed upon it without the intervention of the corporeal senses by which we see, hear, touch, taste, and smell. Memory, like an archive, can store up all kinds of forms and images and present them in turn to the imagination and intellect, where a judgment about them can be made. The interesting thing is that just as any of our five senses can send signals to the inner faculties (for example, the sound of a bell on Saturday morning can remind us of a wedding we attended), so too, "God and devil" can present to these same faculties supernaturally — without exterior stimuli — certain representations. Scripture is replete with Spirit-filled as well as demoniacally perverse examples (cf. *AMC*, II, 16 [3]).

It ought not to be surprising to learn that as one advances in the spiritual life, one may be more prone to receive supernatural imaginative visions. These can affect us for better or worse. That is why they require careful appraisal by a wise master. All might be well were God alone offering the "jewels of images" supernaturally to the intellect. But on this plane the devil also roams, dangerously so. Whereas God can dwell in the soul substantially and impart knowledge to one directly, the demonic may use this means to confuse and misdirect an earnest but naive seeker. After all, false prophets can use their "visions" to seduce followers, as in the infamous Jonestown suicides. Thus St. John takes up the task of instructing the intellect about visions "so that it may not be hindered and impeded by the true ones from union with divine wisdom, nor deceived by the false ones" (*AMC*, II, 16 [5]).

Do Not "Feed" on Visions

Visions, from whatever source they arise, are presented to the mind and memory through a particular image or idea. We must neither "feed" upon them, however, nor "encumber" ourselves with them. The problem is that people starved for some kind of religious experience are prone to find nourishment for their spiritual life in the extraordinary. They are likely to develop a kind of collector's mentality, gathering up accounts of unusual happenings to share with gullible followers.

I remember once being at a religious educators' meeting. After my talk, when I went out into the lobby to have a cup of coffee, a man and a woman approached me. They had not heard the address but had read one of my books in which I discussed the "night of faith." They said that despite what I had written about the rarity of such events, they had many "visions" about the role "God wanted Mabel and me to play in the church." In subdued voices, reduced to a mere whisper, they informed me that they had been appointed by God in one vision to become "exorcists" and that in the past year alone they had personally conducted 375 "exorcisms." What does one do for an encore?, I wondered. It occurred to me that Mabel and Bruce had managed to do in one year more exorcisms than, I suspect, the entire church records!

Don't feed on these visions, St. John cautions. Disencumber yourself from them whether they be false and

diabolical or authentic and of divine origin. If the latter discernment is true, God will give the increase in
the form of obedience, humility, faith, and a sense of
vocation. The fruits of special graces will be shown without your having to boast about them. A sure sign that
you are in danger is your tendency to hoard these experiences. By such an attitude you lose both the poverty of spirit and the purity of heart any true vision
presupposes.

The wisdom of God is without boundaries. It is pure
and simple, not cluttered and complex. Our minds must
emulate this simplicity, remaining insofar as possible
unattached to any particular knowledge bestowed by
images or forms. In the realm of faith, the best knowing
occurs in unknowing, the deepest clarity in obscurity.
However sublime a vision may be, it inevitably limits
God in some manner. God is higher than the highest
mountain, deeper than the deepest sea. He is utterly
limitless. To see him, as it were, we must see through
and beyond all comparisons, likenesses, forms and figures. We must be willing to meet him, as Moses did, in
a cloud of unknowing. St. John gives the reason:

> Manifestly, in this high state of union God does not
> communicate Himself to the soul — nor is this possi-
> ble — through the disguise of any imaginative vision,
> likeness, or figure, but mouth to mouth: the pure and
> naked essence of God (the mouth of God in love) with
> the pure and naked essence of the soul (the mouth of
> the soul in the love of God) (AMC, II, 16 [9]).

In short, we can advance in faith only by closing our
eyes to clear and particular knowledge about God. Any
attempt to reach this essential union that lacks awe for
the Mystery is bound to fail. Any leaning on visions,
as if they could effect union, will end in illusion. It is
better to renounce and avoid such events, for to dwell

too much on them is more likely than not to hinder true advancement.

Cautions to Take into Account

According to the saint, the good effect of the union of love does not depend in any way on admitting or having visions. He believes, to the contrary, that "for the sake of progress . . . one should always deny them" (*AMC*, II, 16 [10]). The knowledge, love, or sweetness they effect, if they are of God, will remain in the soul passively. We can let go of the actual happening as soon as possible and still benefit from being in the presence of God in a memorable way.

St. John counsels us to drop "the wrappings of spiritual communications" in order to ready ourselves to receive "the goods . . . they cause" (*AMC*, II, 16 [11]). It is as if one were to gnaw upon the rind of an orange and miss the sweet pulp within. To pay too much attention to a vision or the particular knowledge it produces would detract us from the spirituality God is infusing in our innermost depths. While concentrating on what a vision means, we may miss the unintelligible and unimaginable horizon to which it points. We may unwittingly bypass an encounter with the Most High granted solely because God loves us and not because of any effort on our part.

Rather than concentrating on the visible "vision," which provides no foundation for faith, our eyes, says St. John, should be fixed on the invisible — on what belongs not to sense but to spirit, on what strengthens pure faith. Ironically, what God grants for the purpose of drawing us forward — a supernatural vision — may become, because of our pride and the need to be special, a blocking of the way. Thus the question naturally arises: "If it is true that God in giving supernatural visions does not want one thereby to desire, lean upon, or pay attention to them, why does He give them at all?" (*AMC*, II, 16 [13]).

St. John expounds on this question in the following chapters, but before doing so he offers a few precautions:

1.   Any sensible communication of the supernatural through visions and forms subjects the "visionary" to numerous dangers and errors. It may impede further progress to pure faith — all because one is ignorant of God's method and purpose in bestowing these visions.

2.   Lacking enlightenment from a wise and balanced spiritual director as to how to behave toward these phenomenon — their divine origin notwithstanding — the "visionary" may become attached to and possessive of them. They are treated in a sense like worldly goods. One admits some as valuable and rejects others as worthless.

3.   A complicated process of discerning ensues, a task God does not impose on the "visionary" at all. According to St. John, God does not desire to expose simple and unlearned people to such a dangerous endeavor.

The bottom line for St. John remains firm. We must close our eyes to any particular knowledge, however sublime, or it will inevitably limit God in some manner by confining the Spirit to a form or image. The only way to advance in faith is by faith alone. The only way to proceed toward the light is in darkness. The only way to move ahead is to wait in the wings. Until the clear vision of God dawns upon the soul, in the daybreak of eternity, the human mind can never penetrate the divine mystery.

Purpose of Spiritual Favors

The question persists: Why does God bestow supernatural favors already in this life? For his response to make sense, St. John must proceed on the basis of three

fundamental principles suggested by the scriptures and
the spiritual masters (cf. *AMC*, II, 17 [2]). Briefly, he assumes that God's words are always well ordered; God's
wisdom disposes all things gently; and God moves each
thing according to its mode.

In moving the soul from one extreme, a corporeal,
sense-dependent state, to another extreme, the state of
divine union, God orders our course gently, according
to the human mode of acquiring knowledge step by step.
God's goal, simply put, is to move us from knowing by
means of sense experience to a spiritual wisdom that
is incomprehensible to the senses. Such would be the
movement, for example, from discursive meditation to
deep interior contemplation.

One is mindful here of St. John's image of God as a
nurturing mother, first offering the child her full breast,
then weaning it from dependency on her, and finally
placing the child on a path of growth where he or she
is free to resist or respond to the mother's voice. The
purpose of God's bestowing these favors is first of all to
encourage us to pursue spiritual wisdom. We do so by
accommodating our senses to the spiritual life by means
of such disciplines as spiritual reading, devotional attention, fasting and abstinence, penance, and the like.
Secondly, by granting to us a few supernatural favors,
gifts, and consolations, God confirms our intention to
do good and to withdraw our appetites from excessive
attachments to anything less than God. These favors are
also bestowed to align our interior senses of imagination and memory, by means of meditation and reflective
reasoning, with more transcendent concerns. Lastly, and
wholly dependent on grace, it is God's purpose to further enlighten our minds through the bestowal of supernatural imaginative visions that reform and refine our
powers of perception and apprehension of the divine.

Though for the sake of analysis St. John traces these happenings step-by-step, he wisely points out that God can operate in any way he chooses. The process depends on what God judges expedient for the soul or upon the favors God wants to confer. Still, on the basis of his experience as a spiritual director, the saint believes that God ordinarily proceeds in the way described here. Like a good teacher, God instructs us by moving from the known to the unknown, from the outer shell to the inner core, from the sensible to the spiritual. The aim is to cultivate sensitivity to the movements of the Spirit in our life to such a degree of refinement that we form a habit or disposition for spiritual things accompanied by a progressive detachment from anything that does not facilitate in some manner our longing for union with God.

Moving from Things of Sense to Those of Spirit

As we move beyond discursive and imaginative meditation, we begin to "taste" the grace of spiritual communion with God. "Voided" are sensory apprehensions pertaining to this wholly transcendent Mystery. Indeed the saint quotes the maxim: *Gustato spiritu, desipit omnis caro* (Once the taste and savor of the spirit is experienced, everything carnal is insipid). He adds: "The ways of the flesh (which refer to the use of the senses in spiritual things) afford neither profit nor delight" (*AMC*, II, 17 [5]). I am reminded here of these wonderful lines from St. John's poem, "Commentary Applied to Spiritual Things," in which he writes in Stanza 3:

> He who is sick with love,
> Whom God Himself has touched,
> Finds his tastes so changed
> That they fall sway
> Like a fevered man's

Who loathes any food he sees
And desires I-don't-know-what
Which is so gladly found.

Advancing in this way, one no longer judges sensate consolations to be essential for the flight to God; in fact the opposite is true. One is led, as it were, from the rind of sense and childish attachment to the hidden fruit of God-initiated and faith-filled spiritual nourishment. This weaning process from the "breast of the senses" to a mature quest for God occurs not according to any human timetable but according to the pace of grace set by God. God brings us — we do not and cannot bring ourselves — to contemplation.

St. John attaches "warning lights," as it were, to any kind of imaginative vision or supernatural communication apprehended by the senses. He firmly counsels, in the strongest possible tone, that we must not even desire to give them admittance, "even though they come from God" (AMC, II, 17 [7]). Understanding human nature as he does, the saint is sure that such phenomena will lead to an imperfection like spiritual pride or to some form of possessiveness ("What! You've never felt the rapture of spiritual ecstasy! How can you call yourself a baptized Christian! Let me tell you exactly what it feels like").

Secondly, to let go of these kinds of experiences is to free ourselves from the task of having to discern which are false and which are true, which come from an angel of light and which from the prince of darkness. St. John sees all such questions, especially for the average person, as a profitless waste of time, a hindrance to true progress, and an occasion of many imperfections. All too often the blind begin to lead the blind on a roller coaster ride from spiritual elation to stagnancy, from floating ecstasy to seemingly depressive everydayness.

Somewhat playfully St. John reminds us in so many words that God takes the risk of teaching our fallen nature how to fly. Instead of letting his Spirit do the leading we rush to take over the controls. God wants us to feast with him at a heavenly banquet and we mistake crumbs and morsels for the main course. God's dream is to give us so much more, but because of our limits in the realm of spirituality, because of our sensory incapacity, we are inclined to settle for much less.

Role of Renunciation

What must we renounce in regard to spiritual goods communicated by means of the senses? In a word, everything. All objects pertaining to the exterior senses that accord so-called supernatural knowledge have to be relinquished. The list includes: "locutions and words to the sense of hearing; visions of saints and beautifully resplendent light to the sense of sight; fragrance to the sense of smell; delightful tastes to the palate; and to the sense of touch other pleasures derived from the spirit" (*AMC*, II, 17 [9]).

Even the content of interior imaginative apprehensions must be subject to the same discipline of detachment. All one can do is to fasten the eyes of the soul "only upon the valuable spirituality they cause." One's aim and that of a good director must be to preserve the fervor awakened by doing all that one does for the service of God. In other words, our role is to cultivate the dispositions of faith, hope, and love without paying much, if any, attention to supernatural representations or sensible gratifications. The reward will be a sustaining encounter with God rather than an empty project of self-sustained salvation. In the words of St. John:

> By this attitude a person takes from these apprehensions only what God wants him to take, that is, the spirit of devotion, since God gives them for no other

principal reason. And he rejects the sensory element which would not have been imparted had he possessed the capacity for receiving spirituality without the apprehensions and exercises of the senses (*AMC*, II, 17 [9]).

Misleading Power of Supernatural Phenomena

So harmful to seekers and directors is this attention to "visions" that St. John strives in several chapters to delineate in unambiguous terms why poor instruction on this path is treacherous for progress. If a spiritual guide is unwise, unlearned and inexperienced, the person being guided risks being improperly directed. Hence, before giving guidance to others, directors should submit themselves to diligent self-scrutiny. The following questions may be pertinent for this purpose:

1. Do I have a bent toward revelations that produce in my soul some effect, pleasure, or satisfaction?

2. Am I aware of how much my enthusiasms affect listeners in a direction relationship?

3. If I detect that the other is more advanced than I, do I strive to bring him or her down to my level because, among other things, I do not want to admit my limits?

4. Do I tend to esteem anything extraordinary that happens to me?

5. Do I fail because of my own enthusiasms to divest disciples of their desire for visions? Do I in fact make the extraordinary a topic of conversation or the main theme of spiritual conferences, dwelling at length on how to discern the true from the false?

6. Do I go so far as to counsel directees to request more of these favors from God as a means of gaining supernatural knowledge?

7. Should such favors be granted for whatever reason, do I accept them as sure signs of God's pleasure, never stopping to consider that God may be displeased by such petitions and prefer that I abide quietly with him in faith and hope?

8. When I discover that I am on the wrong track, when doubts begin to surface about the quality of my direction, do I dismiss them and look instead for evidence that events have come to pass as I predicted?

9. Do I understand how easy it is for even the finest directors to slip into occasional delusion because of the fallen nature all humans share?

10. Do I know that God's revelations are not bound to conform to human expectations? That behind any literal happening is a world of spiritual sense yet to be discerned? That infinite truth escapes finite channels of understanding?

Once these questions are honestly faced, it is possible to understand why we can be and are misled by visions and locutions, to mention only two kinds of supernatural apprehensions. The saint's cautions pertaining to these phenomena emerge from two observations: The first has to do with our defective manner of understanding them; the second with the variability of their causes. What comes from God is of God. The problem resides in the translation, in our feeble attempts to articulate in human language what is profoundly ineffable. This difficulty is increased by the fact that other "spirits" contrary to God can play upon human imagination and cause, as it were, static in the communication. Undoubtedly God in his graciousness does communicate himself to us, but other spirits can evoke similar sensations.

To prove his point St. John turns to a series of examples from the scriptures which illustrate that God

"usually embodies in . . . prophecies, locutions, and revelations other ways, concepts, and ideas remarkably different from the meaning we generally find in them"
(*AMC*, II, 19 [1]). The paradox is that the surer and
more truthful God's self-communications are, the less
true they may seem to human minds receiving them.

St. John cites, among others, the Genesis account of
God telling Abraham that his will is to give him this
land (the land of the Canaanites). Abraham — already
being old — immediately asks God how he will possess
it (cf. Gn 15:7–8). In other words, God speaks from a
divine perspective, but Abraham wants immediate evidence that what God says will be literally and tem-
porally fulfilled. In fact, only Abraham's offspring four
hundred years hence would possess the land. Fortu-
nately for Abraham and his descendants the patriarch
finally understood what God had in mind. His story provides an interesting illustration of the problem St. John
is highlighting, namely, the potential disconnection between what God says and how we interpret it. Being
the "master of suspicion" that he is, St. John is relent-
less in his conclusion that the communication, though
of divine origin, has to be submitted to all too human
hermeneutics, which often despoil its meaning.

Several additional examples are cited: God telling Jacob that if he goes down to Egypt, he will go with him,
lead him out, be his guide (cf. Gn 46:1–4), but Jacob dies
in Egypt; he never returns from there alive (cf. Gn 49:33).
Again the literal prophecy is not fulfilled according to Jacob's timetable, but it is realized in his offspring, for God
does deliver them from Egypt years later. To take this
communication literally would have disillusioned any
listener, for, in fact, God did not fulfill his promise and
bring Jacob out of the land alive. Hence the point has to
be made again by St. John: "Although God's promise in

itself was true, there would have been utter delusion in its interpretation" (*AMC*, II, 19 [3]).

Other stories reveal the same pattern. God promises or foretells something; humans interpret what he is saying; their interpretation is wrong, but God's promise is still fulfilled in a way they did not anticipate or expect. In the Book of Judges, Chapter 20:11–48, God humbles the tribe of Benjamin and only then allows victory to be won. While God's words in themselves are not deceptive, the literal interpretation humans tend to give to locutions and revelations only confers what St. John calls the "outer rind" of the meaning, whereas God wants to express and impart the "elusive, spiritual meaning contained in the words." He adds: "This spiritual meaning is richer and more plentiful than the literal meaning and transcends those limits" (*AMC*, II, 19 [5]).

The issue here is one of interpretation. To remain bound to the letter of the vision or locution is to expose oneself and others to serious error. In the face of any divine communication, one has to wait upon the word in the darkness of faith and allow its spiritual meaning to emerge. This meaning, St. John says, is incomprehensible to the senses; hence it will always escape the verbal or written tools of sensate interpretation.

Eventually, of course, even the spiritual meaning has to be recorded, but the key resides, it would seem, in the word "eventually." To see the deepest meaning of what is going on in the mind of God takes time. Only over the millennia can we humans catch a glimpse of the whole tapestry of truth God is weaving. To live in the meantime in unknowing calls for mature faith. When God speaks in a tongue other than ours, we may not like it; we may feel annoyed. We may be inclined to mock prophets who tell us that the truth lies in the waiting, as the people mocked Isaiah (cf. Is 28:9–11). But that is the way it is. The spiritual meaning is difficult to understand; it escapes our literal, time-bound interpretations. Imagine the frustration of Jeremiah, who, when he mouthed God's promise of peace, could not have known that it referred to the promised Messiah (cf. Jer 4:10). When instead wars and trials came upon the chosen race, it seemed as if God was a deceiver. And still the prophet had to proclaim that all he said was true when in fact everything was turning out contrary to the people's expectations!

As if all of this were not frustrating enough, imagine what happens when one turns from the Old to the New Testament and finds that the One who David said shall reign from sea to sea (cf. Ps 72:8) and will liberate the poor from the power of the mighty (cf. Ps 72:12) is the same Christ who was born in a stable, lived in poverty, and died in misery. Do we not begin to sense anew the depth of the faith St. John challenges us to live? Here we are promised a liberator, we follow him, and our reward is persecution and death for his name's sake!

Spiritually speaking, of course, all of these prophecies come true, for Christ offers us not an earthly kingdom but one that is eternal; he liberates us from the captivity of sin and frees us to enjoy already on earth a foretaste of the freedom that lasts forever. But, blind to the spiritual meaning of his message, even his friends betrayed him. After his resurrection, the message still remained opaque to dull minds bound to literal proofs (cf. Acts 1:6).

Once again St. John reiterates his critique of the delusive powers of human understanding. He says that, compared to our interpretations,

> [God's words and revelations] embody an abyss and
> depth of spiritual significance, and to want to limit
> them to our interpretation and sensory apprehensions
> is like wanting to grasp a handful of air, which will
> escape the hand entirely and leave only a particle of
> dust (AMC, II, 19 [10]).

Application of St. John's
Counsel in Spiritual Direction

What does all of this have to say to spiritual directors? First of all, they should encourage directees in general not to pay heed to supernatural apprehensions — to let them come and go as God wills, for they are only small "particles of spirituality." The best advice is to turn away from visions and locutions and reside in the darkness of faith. Only in faith, according to St. John, is spiritual liberty and plenitude to be obtained. Deep interior purification must precede the art of interpreting God's pronouncements and the practice of spiritual direction. One who is unspiritual simply cannot hope to judge or understand the things of God correctly. Moreover, one always misses the mark if one judges them literally with the tools of sensory apprehension alone.

Let us quote in full one of St. John's most telling examples of what kind of interpretation a spiritual director ought to offer a sincere seeker who experiences a locution.

> A soul has intense desires to be a martyr. God answers, "you shall be a martyr"; and He bestows deep interior consolation and confidence in the truth of this promise. Regardless of the promise, this person in the end does not die a martyr; yet the promise will have been true. Why, then, was there no literal fulfillment? Because the promise will be fulfilled in its chief, essential meaning: the bestowal of the essential love and reward of a martyr. God truly grants the soul the essence of both its desire and His promise, because the formal desire of the soul was not a manner of death, but the service of God through martyrdom and the exercise of a martyr's love for Him. The manner of death in itself is of no value without this love, and God bestows martyrdom's love and reward perfectly by other means. Even though the

individual does not die a martyr, he is profoundly satisfied, since God has fulfilled his desire (*AMC*, II, 19 [13]).

The second issue St. John raises has to do with what happens when we take God's affirmations too literally. Examples from the scriptures (cf. 1 Kgs 21:27–29) reveal that the self-communications of God are not static but dynamic and in dialogue with the listener. A fact may be affirmed, a direction revealed, a parable told, but the outcome of what is affirmed, revealed, or told depends on the person's readiness, on his or her willingness to cooperate with the Holy Spirit at the opportune time to apply the spiritual meaning. As St. John says:

> We should not think, therefore, that because revelations and locutions have a divine origin — and especially if they are dependent on human, changeable causes — they will infallibly eventuate according to their literal meaning (*AMC*, II, 20 [4]).

We are often misled because words that connote familiar meanings may not conform to divine intentions. For instance, what "year" means to us affects our appraisal of any locution or revelation granted to us. Often consultation with a spiritual director is necessary because we cannot rest assured that our appraisal of a supernatural apprehension is the correct or final one. Even the best spiritual guides know they are incapable of comprehending the secret truths, the diverse meanings, of divine pronouncements. Error is always possible. The amazing reality is that God knows our weaknesses and still speaks. So great is his love for us that God cannot but communicate himself to us. This truth alone is reason for sheer awe and abiding faith. No wonder the prophets considered being entrusted to proclaim the word of God a severe trial. Who would not feel unclean of lips and utterly unworthy? (cf. Jer 20:7–9). Even Jonah reached

the point of such anger and frustration that he begged
God to take away his life (cf. Jon 4:1, 3).

> Why, then, should we be surprised if God's locutions
> and revelations do not materialize as expected? Sup-
> pose God affirms or represents to an individual some
> promise (good or bad, pertaining to the person him-
> self or to another); if this promise is based on certain
> causes (devotion or service rendered to God, or of-
> fense committed against Him, now or in the future)
> and these causes remain, the promise will be accom-
> plished. But since the duration of these causes is un-
> certain, the fulfillment of the promise is too. *One should
> seek assurance, therefore, not in understanding but in faith*
> (*AMC*, II, 20 [8], *Italics mine*).

Letting Go of Sensory Signs of God's Love

St. John carries his analysis of supernatural apprehensions a step further by trying to explain why God experiences displeasure in our continual quest for sensory
signs of his love. This is not to say that God ignores our
requests and refuses to reply. It is only to note that this
urgency, this inability to rely on faith alone, may dis-
please, offend, and even anger God, for he so loved us
that he gave his Son for our salvation. Frequently the
scriptures address the danger of our "tempting" God
(cf. Is 7:12), of our desiring that he communicate with
us in extraordinary ways. Why, then, does God answer
such petitions?

The truth is that sometimes the devil answers instead.
If the answer is of God, St. John suggests that it is because God has mercy on our weakness. He knows that
without some sign we may sadden and turn back. So
gracious is our Divine Lover that "He is like a fountain
from which everyone draws as much water as the jug
he carries will hold" (*AMC*, II, 21 [2]). Such actions have
nothing to do with our demands but with what God

judges to be right for us at this stage of our journey. He
may condescend to respond to a simple petition, but this
does not mean he wants us to persist in this practice or
that there is not a better way.

St. John provides a vivid example of what he is saying:

> A father of a family provides at table many different
> kinds of food, some better than the other. One of his
> children will ask for a dish, not of the better food,
> but of the first that meets the eye, and the child will
> do so because it knows how to eat this kind of food
> better than the other. Now when the father observes
> that his child refuses to eat the food offered to it and
> wants and likes only that first dish, he gives it to his
> child sadly so that it will not become unhappy and
> go without its meal. . . .
>
> God accordingly condescends to some souls by
> granting what is not the best for them, because they
> are ignorant of how to journey by any other way.
> Some souls obtain sensible or spiritual sweetness from
> God because they are incapable of eating the stronger
> and more solid food of the trials of the cross of His
> Son. *He would desire them to take the cross more than any
> other thing* (*AMC*, II, 21 [3], *Italics mine*).

The fact that St. John lingers on this matter leads us
to believe that he sees in it a major obstacle to spiritual progress. He considers the desire for knowledge of
things through supernatural means extremely dangerous
— far more so than seeking gratifications in the sensitive part of the soul. He is hard pressed to see how a
person who tries to derive knowledge in this way can
fail to sin. Think for a moment how many people in our
time claim to have access to the supernatural through
seances, palm reading, theories of reincarnation, misdi-
rected charismatic experiences, new age and transper-
sonal psychologies. Such attempts often overlook the
common ways of natural reason and the law and doctrine contained in the gospel and the living tradition of

the church. When and if a supernatural truth seems to be imparted to us, we should receive it with caution. We should brush aside all subjective feelings pertinent to the revelation and examine it objectively, remembering that the devil, in order to delude us, can use empty promises to seduce us from reliance on prayer and hope in God alone. The wise thing to do, especially in times of trial and difficulty, is to follow the gospel and its application in the perennial teaching of the church, to place ourselves in God's hands, and to trust that God will lead us toward what we have been seeking from the start.

Danger of Deception

Focusing further on the reality of demonic seduction in relation to the desire for extraordinary revelations, St. John indicates that the devil can impart "facsimiles of God's communications so that, disguised among the flock like the wolf in sheep's clothing, his meddling may be hardly discernible" (*AMC*, II, 21 [7]; cf. Mt 7:15). The demonic uses conjecture, reasonable manifestations and revelations that "must be from God," together with knowledge of past or future events to carry on this seduction. Hence we must exercise extreme caution in regard to any and all supernatural communications.

Because the devil can craftily insert lies in the midst of "divine lights," the only way to be liberated from his power is to flee these phenomena as such. Not to do so is to risk seduction via our own vanities and phantasies, for the devil plays upon presumption, curiosity, and vainglory. In the name of pursuing the things of God, one ends up showing contempt for them.

The evils of delusion, spiritual darkness, dissention, and confusion breed a spirit of misconstruing everything (cf. Is 19:12). Stubborn, easily seduced people may make their faith dependent on knowing what is ultimately unknowable. Their meddling darkens the light of faith in

which God really wants them to live. As a result, they
necessarily fall into error. They will not listen to anyone who tries to persuade them that what they "see
and hear" may be of diabolical origin. The downward
spiral into delusion speeds up because deception is inevitable when one is out of touch with God. According
to St. John, "The devil then intervenes, answering in harmony with that person's desire and pleasure; and since
the devil's replies and communications are pleasing and
satisfactory, the individual will let himself become seriously deluded" (AMC, II, 21 [13]).

The Way Is Christ

"Behold My Son." This is St. John's response to anyone who desires a word of comfort, an insight into the
secrets of salvation, a glimpse of the wisdom and wonder of God. After giving us his only-begotten Son, what
more could God possibly do for us? What other answer
or revelation of God's could surpass such a communication? What response, then, shall we make:

> Fasten your eyes on Him alone, because in Him I have
> spoken and revealed all, and in Him you shall dis-
> cover even more than you ask for and desire. You are
> making an appeal for locutions and revelations that
> are incomplete, but if you turn your eyes to Him you
> will find them complete. For He is My entire locution
> and response, vision and revelation, which I have al-
> ready spoken, answered, manifested, and revealed to
> you, by giving Him to you as a brother, companion,
> master, ransom, and reward. . . . Hear Him because
> I have no more faith to reveal nor truths to mani-
> fest. . . . You shall not find anything to ask or desire
> through revelations and visions; behold Him well, for
> in Him you will uncover all these revelations already
> made, and many more (AMC, II, 22 [5]).

As St. Paul said, to know Christ and him crucified is
all the wisdom one could hope for and seek (cf.

1 Cor 2:2). Indeed this "is the method of remedying our spiritual ignorances and weaknesses; here we shall find abundant medicine for them all" (*AMC*, II, 22 [7]). So convinced is St. John of this "narrow way" that he declares that we should disbelieve, at least initially, anything communicated in a supernatural manner. We should instead believe more firmly in the teaching of Christ (cf. Gal 1:8) communicated through the church and its lawful authority and the reasoning powers God bestows on the community of the faithful.

In summary, St. John offers directors and directees alike the following excellent counsels:

1.   If you receive any sort of communication through supernatural means, immediately recount it clearly, integrally, and simply to a spiritual director. This does not violate the general rule to be undesirous of these communications, and in fact to reject and pay no attention to them. When such a communication occurs, it is still necessary to seek consultation for three reasons:

— The effect, light, strength, and security of many divine communications are not completely confirmed in your soul until you discuss them with another whom God sets before you as a spiritual judge with the power to bind, loose, approve, and reprove.

— You ordinarily need instruction pertinent to these experiences in order to be guided through the dark night of spiritual deprivation and poverty.

— For the sake of humility, submission, and mortification, you should give a complete account to your director, even if he or she disregards or disesteems communications of this kind.

Central to growth in humility, according to St. John, is a willing submission on the part of a directee to this ordeal. True, you may feel ashamed; you may wish more than anything to pay no attention to what has happened and to dismiss as unnecessary having to share this moment with a director. But actually what you suffer in doing so can only serve to increase your humility.

2.   To directors, St. John has this to say: Just because he has stressed the importance of rejecting these communications and their duty to forbid souls to make them a topic of conversation, does not mean that they are to show severity, displeasure, or scorn in dealing with them. Directors must remember that God may in fact be leading souls by these means. There is no reason at the onset of the telling to oppose a directee or to become frightened or scandalized by what he or she is recounting. Instead, you should be kind and peaceful, encouraging and supportive, so the recipient will tell what has occurred in as clear and honest a way as possible.

3.   The result is that good spiritual directors will guide directees on the way of faith; they will offer them excellent instructions on how to turn from supernatural communications as such to meet more intimately the God of love toward whom they point.

There is no doubt in St. John's mind that "one act done in charity is more precious in God's sight than all the visions and communications possible — since they imply neither merit nor demerit — and . . . many who have not received these experiences are incomparably more advanced than others who have had many" (AMC, II, 22 [19]). Whatever else transpires in a person's life, the intellect must be liberated from attachment to these apprehensions and directed in the night of faith to that secret light which enkindles the heart with love. Thus: "In all things, both high and low, let God be your goal, for in no other way will you grow in merit and perfection" (Degrees of Perfection, No. 8).

6

Spiritual Apprehensions and the Night of Faith

(Book Two, Chapters 23 to 32, of the *Ascent*)

Only faith can guarantee the blessings that we hope for, or prove the existence of realities that are unseen (Heb 11:1).

Visions, revelations, locutions, and *spiritual feelings* — however authentic these experiences may be — must be submitted to the stark detachment, the *nada,* of the night of faith. St. John never wavers from this position, even though these apprehensions are purely spiritual in nature. None of them is communicated to the intellect through the corporeal senses as such; they are not "imaginary" but "intellectual." They are imparted directly to the recipient without the mediation of any exterior or interior bodily sense. One receives them at once, as it were, clearly, distinctly, supernaturally — without the least bit of effort on the recipient's part. His or her role is not active but passive or, better still, wholly receptive. What occurs is "spiritually visible" to the soul and "intelligible to the intellect" (cf. *AMC,* II, 23 [2]).

While these apprehensions in the widest sense are all "visions" beheld by the "spiritual eye of the soul," certain distinctions analogous to bodily functions are applicable. According to St. John, the term "vision" designates whatever the intellect receives in a manner resembling sight; "revelation" refers to new truths the intellect gains as though by learning and understanding; "locution" signifies whatever is received in a way similar to that of hearing; and "spiritual feelings" encompass all that is perceived after the manner of the other senses, for example, on the supernatural plane a sweet fragrance, savor or delight (cf. AMC, II, 23 [3]). He explains:

> The intellect derives knowledge or spiritual vision from all these communications, without the apprehension of any form, image, or figure of the imagination or natural fantasy. For these experiences are bestowed immediately upon the soul through a supernatural work and means (AMC, II, 23 [3]).

These gifted moments are to be trusted more than corporeal or imaginary experiences of the transcendent. The more interior an apprehension is, the less exposed it may be to the "devil's meddlesomeness" (AMC, II, 23 [4]). The least active we are the better. Still lack of caution may draw even the spiritually gifted to the threshold of deception. Thus, as we might expect, St. John applies to these four kinds of apprehensions the same counsel afforded all other supernatural phenomena: They are to be neither the object nor the aim of our desire; faith in God alone must be our goal.

With this caution in mind, we shall proceed to explore, with the saint as our guide, the inner workings of the spiritual life, beginning with the first category.

Description of Visions

What do we see? There are two possibilities described by St. John. First of all, a person might "see" and "record" as did John the Evangelist in the twenty-first chapter of the Book of Revelation a vision dealing with literal or symbolic images of heaven and earth — things that are literally absent from the bodily sense of sight but nonetheless present to the spiritual "eye" of the mind. The evangelist describes "the heavenly Jerusalem" by utilizing earthly symbols that at most can only approximate the spiritual reality he is trying to convey in mundane words.

Secondly, visions can encompass incorporeal substances that have no earthly counterpart as such but are "seen" in another higher light, namely, the "light of glory." Such would be a "vision" of angelic hosts — a vision no mortal can really behold and live. At most one might catch a transient glimpse, a passing breeze (cf. 3 Kgs 19:13), a rare moment, when God — for reasons God alone knows — may dispense momentarily with the laws of nature while preserving the life of the individual seer. Still St. John is cautious. He quotes the Exodus text to the effect that no person can see the face of God and live (cf. Ex 33:20). He stresses the rarity of these occasions and insists that they are granted only to persons strong in the spirit of the church and upholders of God's law — persons like Elijah, Moses, and St. Paul. For example, during his experience of divine self-communication on the Damascus Road, Paul knew not whether he was in the body or out of the body (cf. 2 Cor 12:2, 4).

Rare as these occurrences of intellectual vision may be, they bestow more clarity and a greater delicacy of awareness of God than do visions of corporeal substances. Perhaps because strong souls are often asked by God to teach others, God grants them, if only for a brief duration, a vision of what *is* in the deepest sense. St. John explains:

> Suppose that a door were opened so that the soul could see as it would if a flash of lightning were to

illumine the dark night and momentarily make objects
clearly and distinctly visible, only to leave them all in
darkness again. . . [so] the objects seen in that light are
so impressed on [the soul] that as often as it adverts
to them it beholds them as it did before, just as the
forms reflected in a mirror are seen as often as one
looks in it (*AMC*, II, 24 [5]).

Though in the course of time the precise objects of the
vision may grow remote, the impression made on the
soul by them can never be removed. These visions or
infusions from God instill such lasting effects in the soul
as "quietude, illumination, gladness resembling that of
glory, delight, purity, love, humility, and an elevation
and inclination toward God" (*AMC*, II, 24 [6]). These
effects may be more or less intense; one or the other
may predominate — it all depends on what God wills
for the recipient.

One problem in the discernment process cannot be
overlooked and that is the fact that the devil can also
cause these visions to occur in the soul. For example,
during his forty days in the desert, Jesus was shown
by Satan the kingdoms of the world and their glory (cf.
Mt 4:8), but he did not succumb to the temptation to
usurp power; he chose instead to adhere to the will of
the Father.

Effects of Visions

There is, according to St. John, one great difference
between visions diabolical or divine in origin and this
resides in the *effects* they produce. Visions belonging to
the devil will result in the long run in spiritual dryness, an inclination to self-aggrandizement or distorted
self-esteem, a tendency to consider oneself increasingly
important as distinct from enhancing humility, self-
forgetfulness, and only loving God. Diabolical visions
do not produce clarity but confusion; they have no lasting effect but are soon obliterated from experience, thus

tempting the beholder to seek and induce the next "spiritual thrill." In short, "The memory of them is considerably arid, and unproductive of the love and humility caused by the remembrance of the good visions" (*AMC*, II, 24 [7]).

What conclusions can be drawn thus far from St. John's reflections on "visions"? First, even if they are of divine origin, they cannot serve as a proximate means for union with God. God is more than any vision, no matter how profound and efficacious it may be. The only proximate means to union, as the saint consistently teaches, is faith. Thus one must exercise toward these phenomena the "nada" to which St. John always returns.

His counsel, in other words, is this: Don't store up or treasure in any inordinate way the images these visions may impress upon your soul. Desire not to cling to them. Journey beyond what your mind knows to God who is beyond all knowing. This is the only safe path. St. John adds:

> Even if the remembrance of these visions really does stir the soul to some contemplation and love of God, denudation, pure faith, and darkness regarding them will stir and elevate it much more, and without its knowing how or whence this elevation comes (*AMC*, II, 24 [8]).

The point is that love will be enkindled *without our knowing how*; faith will be infused and rooted more deeply in the soul *without our knowing how*; through emptiness, darkness, and nakedness regarding all things, through poverty of spirit, the charity of God will flood the driest regions of the heart *without our knowing how*. Hence:

> The more one desires darkness and annihilation of himself regarding all visions, exteriorly or interiorly receivable, the greater will be the infusion of faith and

consequently of love and hope, since these three the-
ological virtues increase together (*AMC*, II, 24 [8]).

To offer a paraphrased summary of this counsel, it is
as if St. John is saying: This infusion of virtue does not
always register with felt tenderness in the senses. Rather
it endows your soul with strength, greater courage, and
more daring than before. At times the love between you
and God may enkindle a gentle feeling, a warm glow,
but don't mistake the feeling for the reality to which it
points. Most of the time you won't feel or see anything.
All you will know is that you experience more love, happiness, and joy than before. You possess more fortitude.
You are less inclined to shy away from mortification.
You are willing to wait upon God in silence and detachment from creaturely addictions — even the "addiction"
to visions. Whether or not you see or feel anything special, you center your love totally upon God who is and
remains incomprehensible to the human mind.

In conclusion, to quote St. John directly:

> Even if a person is so shrewd, humble, and strong that
> the devil is unable to deceive him by these visions or
> make him (as he usually does) fall into any presump-
> tion, *the visions will be an obstacle to his advancement if he
> fails to practice this denial*, since they impede spiritual
> nudity, poverty, and emptiness in faith — *the requisite
> for union with God* (*AMC*, II, 24 [9], *Italics mine*).

Description of Revelations

Simply understood, a revelation is the disclosure of a
hidden truth. It may take the form of a prophecy, as in
the oracles of an Isaiah or a Jeremiah. It brings into the
light some dark secret or mystery. God himself imparts
some truth to the intellect, some glimpse, beyond our
capacity to know, of divine past, present or future deeds.

St. John defines the existence of two main kinds of
revelation (cf. *AMC*, II, 25 [2]): the disclosure of truths,

notions, and concepts to the intellect, including knowledge of creatures, and the manifestation of divine secrets and hidden mysteries to the inner eye of the soul.

Intellectual Knowledge of the Creator. How does it happen that God can directly bestow upon our minds an understanding of temporal and spiritual things? In the face of such naked truths, how are we to respond? Before answering, St. John prays that God will move his hand as he takes up his pen, for what is imparted to the soul by grace is beyond anything words can hope to convey. Still he will try to explain what happens, albeit in a brief and restricted way.

The truth in question pertains to knowledge of our Creator and to ourselves as his creatures. These revelations, in St. John's words, bring incomparable delight to the soul, for God himself is the direct object of this knowledge. Revealed in all its ineffable beauty, actually experienced, is one of his attributes like omnipotence or goodness. Once revealed this moment remains fixed in and indeed transfixes the soul.

A revelation like this (cf. Ex 34:6–7 and 2 Cor 12:4) never deals with particular things since it discloses the One Supreme Principle. It can only be received by a person who has arrived at union with God, for "It consists in a certain touch of the divinity produced in the soul, and thus it is God himself who is experienced and tasted there" (*AMC*, II, 26 [5]). So sublime and lofty is this experience that the devil cannot meddle with it; he cannot infuse a savor and delight like it; he cannot counterfeit anything so lofty as a taste of the divine essence, a touch of eternal life. Though the devil can play on the surface of the soul and proffer a sensation of grandeur, no diabolical communication can enter the soul's substance and enamor it as does a divine touch.

What are these "touches" like? St. John cannot say enough about them. What they produce in the substance

of the soul is so enriching, for example, "that one of
them would be sufficient not only to remove definitively
all the imperfections which the soul would have been
unable to eradicate throughout its entire life, but also to
fill it with virtues and blessings from God" (AMC, II,
26 [6]).

Mindful of the saying, "One picture is worth a thousand words," it would seem that, according to St. John
of the Cross, one sweet, intimate, and delightful touch of
God is worth any amount of suffering we might have to
undergo for Christ's sake. Revelation in this sense makes
adversity endurable. The faint-hearted experience new-
found courage. Not to suffer for Christ becomes paradoxically a kind of suffering. This sublime knowledge
of God's ultimately benevolent love is unattainable by
human works or efforts; it is a pure gift of grace freely
revealed, transcending what is naturally attainable, not
comparable to other contents of the intellect or imagination. This is an act of "amazing grace," for "God effects
in the soul what it is incapable of acquiring" (AMC, II,
26 [8]).

The question is when and how does such an event
occur? Is there any pattern for this mystery of disclosure? At most St. John can offer a few observations.
These "divine touches," these momentary yet unforgettable remembrances of the "More Than," occur when one
least expects or thinks of them. Like a cool breeze on a
clammy night, like the sight of a garden of roses con-
jured up by a single bloom, so unfolds the story of love
divine: God seeking out the wayward soul and calling
her home as a knight serenades his fair lady and wins
her heart. The melody of love is unmistakably heard
amidst a cacophony of discordant sounds.

These touches, says St. John, are not ethereal but sensible, so much so that they may cause the body to tremble.
Yet they are also still as a mountain lake, so delightful

and refreshing that they may appear to bypass sensations and resonate only in the tranquil depths of the soul. Perhaps the difference could be likened to new love, enervating and attractive, and the affection of old couples, steady and sure, though not lacking in wonder.

Are there other occasions of disclosure through the power of divinely communicated directives? One privileged opening can be found in sacred scripture. For example, Anthony of Egypt fled the city and made his way into the desert because he heard the gospel in his heart and acted immediately on Christ's call to discipleship. Similarly Augustine obeyed the voice of a child, took up the Bible, and decided once and for all to shed the false cloak of concupiscence and put on the Lord Jesus Christ. Later in history Teresa of Avila read Augustine's *Confessions* and decided that it was useless any longer to resist her vocation to reform the Carmelite order.

Naturally, these revelations vary in degree of efficacy. The preceding are examples from the lives of saints who were compelled by grace to conversion of heart. Previously they had been too weak to say yes to God. Now revelation changes that. History attests in their case that one divine touch can and does radically transform even the most recalcitrant soul. No preaching about Christ, no learned discourse about the Word made flesh, could have turned their human weakness into divinely sustained strength. It took a personal encounter with God to change their heart.

Grace vanquished the fortress of pride and produced in St. Paul a new person ready to defend the revelation at the cost of his life. What happened on the Damascus Road was not a question of Saul's deciding to listen or not. At this moment "amazing grace" transcended the exercise of his free will and imparted the knowledge this future teacher of the faith needed, whether he was ready to receive it or not (cf. Acts 9:1–6).

At this level of spiritual maturity, one should not be troubled about desiring or not desiring further transformation. One should simply remain humble and resigned to the flow of grace. Concern of any sort is useless because "God will do His work at the time and in the manner He wishes" (*AMC*, II, 26 [9]).

Certainly it would be as extreme to negate this knowledge as it would be to negotiate with God to bestow it. If there are any prerequisites involved for such graced union, these would include the dispositions of detachment, humility, persecution for love's sake, and resignation to the divine will in consolation and desolation, in aspiration and aridity. Any posture of possessiveness or pride on the part of the pilgrim soul despoils God's plan. He gives these gifts not because we deserve them but because he loves us. When we love him in great detachment for his own sake, God cannot resist, it would seem, revealing himself more intimately to us.

Intellectual Knowledge of Creatures. According to St. John, this kind of knowledge is at once *interior*, or so embedded in the soul by the Holy Spirit that it produces certitude, and *inferior* since it pertains to the truth of things, of deeds and events that, being created, are thereby less than or inferior to God. Still one cannot be dissuaded from what one has beheld of God's glory. In fact one would be inclined to defend, even to the death, what one *knows* to be true. Witness the epiphanic presence of martyrs and spiritual masters, of persons graced with the gift of prophecy and the capacity to discern "spirits" (cf. 1 Cor 12:10).

Despite the efficacy and clarity of the knowledge granted to us, despite the firmness of our interior assent and conviction that this "word" is from the living God, in this arena, cautions St. John, we must be willing to obey the instructions and counsels of a good spiritual director. Humble obedience must prevail, even if the director's advice is contrary to what we feel. What matters is not the knowledge received but the spirit of faith in which we receive it, for in the end we are led by faith to divine union, by believing more than by understanding.

Unwavering as this principle is, it does not preclude instances where through God's grace one receives in a supernatural infused manner true knowledge of existing things (cf. Wis 7:17–21). Solomon received the gift of wisdom. Paul acknowledged the reception of the gifts of prophecy, understanding of tongues, and interpretation of words. The key to discerning whether or not these gifts are truly of God and not the result of willful illusion or demonic seduction depends on the depth, sincerity, and humility of the receiver's grace-filled and purified spirit. The reality is that idolatrous prophets can exist side by side with giants of light and prudence.

In the history of Christianity, the "desert tradition" provides many examples of gifted spiritual directors who could discern true from false spirits, who could read the minds and hearts of those who came to them for counsel. The desert fathers and mothers moved past exterior gestures and verbal disclosures to the inner state of the disciple's soul. Thus were they able to give seekers a word by which to live their life. Anthony of Egypt had this gift. He, more than most, also knew how subtly the devil could slip into these deliberations. Hence he preaches the need for continual prayer and the humble readiness to renounce even knowledge of divine things at the slightest sign of pride and lack of inner purity.

Again, the question arises, when and how does this knowledge occur? Without doubt it enters passively into the soul, thereby excluding any active endeavor. As St. John explains, a person may be distracted and inattentive when suddenly, for apparently no reason, "a keen understanding of what he is hearing or reading will

be implanted in his spirit, an understanding far clearer
than that conveyed through the sound of the words"
(*AMC*, II, 26 [16]). The interesting thing is that while
one may fail to grasp the sense of the words, almost as
if they were in a foreign language, their meaning is still
understood. Here, too, great caution must be exercised,
for the devil can and does deceive persons who do not
remain humble. He can, for instance, instill in one a spirit
of envy that spots the "evil" in the person envied and
righteously feels obliged to put her in her proper place,
going so far as to "publish" her sins. The devil thrives
on defamation, deception, and distress, on any form of
pride posing as humility.

St. John admits that in his own life he had painful personal evidence of what it is like to be nearly destroyed
by "brothers" acting on "divine knowledge," for his own
friars imprisoned him in Toledo in 1577 for his involve-
ment in the Carmelite Reform. Thus he concludes that
this kind of insight, whether or not it is of God, will be
of minuscule benefit if one is attached to it and, in fact,
can be the occasion of serious harm and error.

> A person should [therefore] be extremely careful al-
> ways to reject this knowledge, and he should desire
> to journey to God by unknowing. . . . The director
> should allow the soul to relate this experience briefly,
> but should not make it the main factor in the soul's
> journey toward union with God (*AMC*, II, 26 [18]).

Secret Knowledge. Over the course of time, to mystics,
masters, prophets, and ordinary people, God has disclosed a knowledge of himself and his works that com-
prises what is commonly called "the revelation." This
includes first and foremost our knowledge of God as
a Triune Mystery, as three persons, Father, Son, and
Holy Spirit, in one God. Under the same category are to
be found articles of the Catholic faith, prophecies, and
many other facts — unique and universal — that appear

in the scriptures and become part of our system of belief. These disclosures often occur indirectly — not by word only but via certain signs, figures, images, and likenesses granted to whomever God wills, portending the future or proving anew what has been previously told. Good examples can be found in the *Showings* of Julian of Norwich or the *Dialogue* of St. Catherine of Siena. St. Teresa of Avila describes in the *Book of Her Life* several instances of such divine self-communication.

These holy women are aware of the ways in which this knowledge can contribute toward or be a hindrance to union with God because all three experienced that the demonic can counterfeit the truth, play on human pride, and meddle with already existing articles of faith. Here a person must fall back upon the body of knowledge preserved by the church and never rely on so-called private revelations alone. It is best in such cases to adhere simply to the doctrine of the church. "Let this be kept in mind," says St. John: "Even if there is actually no danger of deception to the soul, a person should be undesirous of knowing the truths of faith clearly, that he [she] may thereby conserve pure and entire the merit of faith and also pass through this night of intellect to the divine light of union" (*AMC*, II, 27 [5]).

Without this reliance on humble faith as one's first priority, it is impossible for even the finest mystic to go undeceived, to say nothing of a beginner. St. John is adamant in his assessment of what must be done, especially in regard to revelations impertinent to the faith.

> The pure, cautious, simple, and humble soul should resist and reject revelations and other visions with as much effort and care as it would extremely dangerous temptations; for in order to reach the union of love there is no need of desiring them, but rather [a great need] of rejecting them (*AMC*, II, 27 [6]).

Even if there were no danger of deception, St. John says in effect, be on your guard against "new" disclosures that deviate however slightly from time-tested truths of faith. Only then, in the night, can you continue your journey to union purely and without error.

Description of Locutions

Supernatural communications or locutions are infused apprehensions "heard" in the inmost heart or soul of spiritual persons without the use or mediation of their bodily senses as such. St. John's intention in describing them is not to attract undue attention to their importance, for nothing of this sort is essential to divine union. As he stresses again and again, the goal of the spiritual life surpasses all natural and supernatural apprehensions and the potential for deception inherent in them. As always, pure faith remains the sole means to oneness with God. Still it is important that disciples and masters know exactly what is going on when such "locutions" occur, for they may occasion, as do all supernatural phenomena, profit or harm to the soul.

According to St. John, locutions fall into three classes. They can be "successive," meaning that words and reasonings are formed and deduced successively in the core of one's being, usually while one is in a state of recollection. Locutions may also be "formal," that is to say, the spirit receives certain distinct words whether or not one is recollected. These "words" come not from oneself but from "another party." Thirdly and most to be trusted are "substantial" locutions comprised of words that are also produced formally in the spirit, whether one is in a recollected state or not. The difference is that these "words" effect in the substance of the soul the same power, the very meaning, they signify (cf. *AMC*, II, 28 [2]).

Successive Locutions. Let me take the liberty of paraphrasing St. John's description of this class of "inner words." Imagine that your spirit is recollected (literally "gathered together") and that you are attentively absorbed in appraising, for example, your vocational call. You reason pro and con about your pending decision, moving quietly from thought to thought, relaxed and open while forming in your mind precise words and judgments. Somewhere in the process of deduction, you seem to sense, with ease and clarity, hitherto unknown truths. It actually seems as if *you* are doing nothing, as if Another is answering and teaching you point by point or successively. You are using your reason in the process, to be sure, but it is as if you are also engaged in a dialogue. A kind of question-and-answer give-and-take appears to be occurring between your intellect as instrument and the Holy Spirit as guide. The Spirit helps you to form true and exact concepts, words, and judgments that you could never have found on your own in such an effortless, yet active way.

Because the truth of God's will for your life is the subject of your thought, you are already present to the Spirit of truth who communes with you, simultaneously giving form to what you are perusing and appraising. Yet a shift has occurred: It is no longer only you who is involved in the process; the Holy Spirit now acts as your teacher, leading the way and giving light, allowing new propositions to emerge (cf. *AMC*, II, 29 [1]).

If you have had an experience like the one St. John describes, you cannot accept that this kind of comprehension originates in you alone. You know that you have been inspired and illumined by the Holy Spirit. There is a problem, however, in this process. It resides not in Spirit-inspired communications, which cannot deceive the mind, but in the words and propositions the humanly weak intellect deduces from these encounters in the translation process. A transfocal directive is usually delicate and subtle; the focal mind because of its limited capacity to "language" what is beyond words cannot completely formulate what it has heard within. As a result, statements about successive locutions tend always to be defective and may even prove false. The complexity, as St. John sees it, is this:

> Since the intellect afterwards joins its own lowly capacity and awkwardness to the thread of truth it had already begun to grasp, it easily happens that it changes the truth in accordance with this lowly capacity; and all as though another person were speaking to it (*AMC*, II, 29 [3]).

Think of how many times people have planted the seed of heresy by taking partial truths, disclosed to them "by the Holy Spirit," and making of these "words" the *whole* truth for all. What St. John describes as happening in his time certainly transpires in our own:

> If any soul whatever after a bit of meditation has in its recollection one of these locutions, it will immediately baptize all as coming from God and with such a supposition say, "God told me," "God answered me." Yet this is not so, but, as we pointed out, these persons themselves are more often the origin of their locution (*AMC*, II, 29 [4]).

The problem of deception compounds the more a person desires to have locutions and to be set apart as someone special that the Holy Spirit, or other saints or angels, has chosen as a channel of divine disclosures. One can become excessively attached to these communications and fail to practice the restraint required to prevent vanity of speech and pride of soul. Without humility and detachment, one risks thinking that something extraordinary has occurred, that God himself has spoken at the slightest inner stirring. In fact nothing has happened but a flight of fancy that engenders no solid fruit, no increase in charity, simplicity, and silence. By paying undue attention to these inner voices, one is drawn far from the abyss of faith, from a quieting of the analytical mind so that one can proceed in darkness to divine love.

Paradoxically, the profit produced by a successive locution will not be received by focusing your attention on it (for to do so is to drive the locution away), but by letting it go and simply applying your will to God in love and surrender. Then the divine communication can be what it is: supernatural and passively received by the intellect, not the result of copious interior reasonings in which human cleverness predominates and the demonic meddles.

Such would be the danger when as soon and as frequently as "it" happens, one runs to write the locution down or to dictate it to others. This kind of attention only serves to induce vainglory. In fact the opposite stance ought to have priority, namely, we are "to give importance to nothing other than sincere effort, the establishment of [our] wills in humble love, and suffering in imitation of the life and mortifications of the Son of God" (*AMC*, II, 29 [9]). Excessive attachments to interior locutions leave one wide open to temptation, for the devil can use inner words and ideas to deceive the intellect and bring one to the brink of serious error, if not total ruin. Behind many desires, after all, stands an avalanche of false arguments.

In summary, then, successive locutions can originate in the intellect from any of the following three causes: the Holy Spirit, who moves and illumines the intellect; the natural light of the intellect as such; and the devil, who uses the power of suggestion to counterfeit true inspiration. How do we know which cause is which? St. John offers the following counsel:

1. When, together with the words and concepts being formed, you love God and simultaneously experience this love with humility and reverence, this may be an indication that the Holy Spirit is working within your

contemplative mind. For, as always, the test of divine inspiration resides not in the felt experience as such but in the charity that flows from it.

2. If your intellect happens to be vivacious, if lights go on all the time without any accompanying exercise of virtue to speak of, then it is likely that the source of "locutions" is actually your own mind. You understandably enjoy the knowledge and light derived from these discoveries, yet after the meditation your will to virtue remains the same or perhaps altogether dry. St. John is quick to explain that locutions arising from the Holy Spirit are not followed by aridity, unless God so ordains for the benefit of the soul, but by deeper abandonment to the will of God and an increase of virtue.

3. Locutions caused by the devil are difficult to discern but generally they leave the will in dryness, diminishing one's pure love of God. Vanity and distorted self-esteem may increase or one may fall into religious complacency, concluding on basis of "locutions" received that he or she has really "made it" on the road to spiritual maturity. Pride may also pose as humility, fervor for God as disguised self-love. It may even be difficult for a truly mature spiritual person to recognize the demonic ploy of fixing in souls excessive attachments to the extraordinary and a slew of false virtues. The devil is adept at trickery. For example, "he is expert at inducing the flow of tears from the feelings he introduces." The reason these seductions attain success is that the tempter moves "the will toward an esteem for these interior communications so that it might . . . occupy itself with things that instead of increasing the virtues occasion the loss of what is already possessed" (*AMC*, II, 29 [11]).

From these considerations pertaining to the delusion and hindrance to spiritual progress locutions can cause, St. John offers an oft-to-be-repeated, stark and simple conclusion: *Pay no heed to them.* Be interested only in firmly directing your will through them toward God. Carry out God's law and holy counsels perfectly. Be content with knowing mysteries and truths in the simplicity and verity with which the church proposes them. In short, *do not pry into profundities and curiosities in which danger is seldom lacking* (cf. AMC, II, 29 [12], *Italics mine*).

Formal Locutions. These "inner words" produced supernaturally in the human spirit are given to one independently without spiritual recollection or the use of the senses. It is as if another person formally utters a word to your heart without the intervention of your mind. Mentally you may be far away from any thought of what you now "hear." Whereas successive locutions involve meditation, formal locutions transcend self-initiated thoughts. They come, as it were, from another source.

Sometimes the words heard are explicit; at other times they are more obscure. They are like whispers spoken to the spirit in reply perhaps to an unvoiced prayer. Maybe they consist of one word, maybe more. Their duration could be prolonged or relatively brief. Underlying these differences in communication is the common fact that these words arise without our doing anything in particular to evoke them; all we have to do is to be receptive to them, as if another person were speaking to us.

According to St. John of the Cross, these locutions are given for three reasons: to teach us more about the plan of God in our life, to shed light on a divine truth already revealed, and to issue a divine command, however contrary and even initially repugnant it may seem to the one receiving it (cf. Ex 3:10–22 and 4:1–18 for Moses' response).

When God is the cause of the locution, its effect is spontaneously efficacious. One finds strength to obey and augment God's command despite the difficulty, humanly speaking, that may be involved. The operable disposition on our side is humility, though God often imparts to the lowly the facility and readiness to do good and the honor thus attained.

By contrast, if the origin of the locutions is diabolical, they will only serve to enhance what brings personal honor to us. We will experience increased resistance to performing any unrewarded task. Social and ecclesiastical climbers are on the top of St. John's list of people whom God finds "abhorrent" in this regard. The devil always slips in when our main motivation for doing good is to call attention to ourselves.

How should we respond, therefore, to formal locutions? The saint's answer should come as no surprise: "A person should *pay no* more *attention to* all *these formal locutions* than he should to the other kind, for besides occupying the spirit with matters irrelevant to faith, . . . they will make him an easy victim of the devil's deceits" (*AMC*, II, 30 [5], *Italics mine*). For safety's sake, we should submit anything inwardly communicated to a wise and discerning spiritual master who will give counsel and decide what is to be done. It is difficult for us to determine on our own if the source of a locution is a good or bad spirit, since its effects can be deceiving. Until such an expert can be found, it is best for the recipient to remain in a posture of resignation and negation. In short, we are to pay no heed to the locution whatsoever. If an experienced counselor is not available, St. John believes it is better *not* to speak of these locutions to anyone. They can be a source of "strange and subtle deceits" to all concerned. Hence: "It should be kept in mind that a person must never follow his own opinion, nor do or admit anything told to him through these locutions, without ample advice and counsel from another" (*AMC*, II, 30 [6]).

Substantial Locutions. What St. John has taught about "formal" locutions is relevant for "substantial" because they too are impressed formally in the soul. There is, however, a significant difference. It resides primarily in their effect, which happens to be, in St. John's words, "vital and substantial." He gives the following examples to make clear the distinction:

> If our Lord should say formally to the soul: "Be good," it would immediately be substantially good; or if He should say: "Love Me," it would at once have and experience within itself the substance of the love of God; or if He should say to a soul in great fear: "Do not fear," it would without delay feel ample fortitude and tranquillity (*AMC*, II, 31 [1]).

These words are indeed full of power and hence can produce *substantially* in the soul the exact meaning of what is said and the necessary action. "God did this to Abraham," says St. John, "for when He said: *Walk in my presence and be perfect* (Gn 17:1), Abraham immediately became perfect and always proceeded with reverence for God." The same "power of the Word" is observable in the gospel. When Jesus uttered a prayer or a command, he healed the sick, raised the dead, and cast out demons from the possessed.

Unlike the two previous classes, successive and formal, to which we were warned not to pay attention, St. John believes that this one is both important and valuable. Substantial locutions impart "life, virtue, and incomparable blessings" to the soul. In fact, says the saint, "A locution of this sort does more good for a person than a whole lifetime of deeds."

How is one to behave or respond to such a gratuitous encounter with the living God? There is, in fact, nothing to be done, for God bestows these divine self-communications on whomsoever God chooses in order to accomplish in the soul what the words themselves express. There is nothing for you to desire or refrain from desiring, for your wish, especially in this regard, is not and can never be God's command nor can any human want or resistance hinder the divine effect. All you can do is to remain resigned to God's will in a posture of humility. There is nothing for you to reject, for the effect of the locution will always be substantiated in the soul and be replete with holy blessings. Since reception is passive, any activity on your side would be superfluous.

Finally, there is nothing to fear because no demonic deceit is possible if a locution is truly substantial. Neither the intellect nor the devil can intervene in this communication, short of a person voluntarily entering into a pact with the Evil One! While the demonic can impress confused suggestions upon the mind and even arouse evil effects in the guise of the good, in this case the devil is utterly "unable to produce effects similar to those arising from God's locutions, for there is no comparison between God's words and the devil's" (*AMC*, II, 31 [2]). God's words are like fire and the hammer that breaks rocks (cf. Jer 23:28–29). The paltry powers of the demonic fade to dust in comparison to divine locutions.

St. John concludes that substantial communications from God are a great aid to divine union. The more interior and substantial they are, the more good we stand to gain from them. Surely there is no happier and humble person than the one to whom God speaks directly. Such locutions change the course of salvation history. They bring giants of spirituality like Abraham and Samuel, Peter and Paul, to their knees. They make Francis and Clare of Assisi, Teresa of Avila, and John of the Cross, and countless known and unknown saints instruments of a providential plan only those who are poor in spirit can hope to see. No wonder St. John concludes this portion of the *Ascent* with the firm assurance: "Happy the soul to whom God speaks these substantial words."

Description of Spiritual Feelings

In his analysis of apprehensions communicated supernaturally to the soul St. John turns in the final chapter of Book Two to "spiritual feelings." These are of two kinds: affections of the will and divine touches, delights, and consolations in the substance of the soul.

Those in the will are sublime when they originate in God but those felt in the substance of the soul are extremely lofty and exceptionally advantageous. It is not easy to know the origin of these feelings or the reason God bestows them. While good works dispose the soul to receive such divine gifts and favors, their bestowal does not depend on what we do nor on the way in which we meditate. That God may touch you when receiving this gift is the farthest thing from your mind. The touch may be distinct and of short duration or not so distinct but longer lasting. The point is that God grants these touches to whom God wills and for reasons God alone knows.

For clarity's sake, St. John says that these feelings are not allied to the intellect as much as to the will. However, the apprehension, knowledge, and understanding associated with them overflows, so to speak, into the intellect, imparting a sublime and delightful perception of God. This same effect is true of both affections in the will and touches in the substance of the soul, whether they are sudden or lasting. This new understanding of God is "apophatic." It cannot be given a name nor can one exactly explain the feeling from which it overflows. What matters is that the intellect should refrain from meddling into these sublime communications with its natural curiosity and effective bent.

The best one can do is to remain receptive to God in pure and passive faith without any active effort. Otherwise one risks erroneous interpretations based on human knowledge which is always limited and, worse than this,

subject to falling prey to the false knowledge prompted
by the devil. The posture to maintain is one of "resignation, humility, and passivity" (*AMC*, II, 32 [4]). When
God beholds that a person is humble and unpossessive,
a divine stirring may be granted. One may be led by
the Spirit beyond touches of union to the divine touch-
stone from whom all true supernatural apprehensions
and pure faith proceed in the first place.

7

Union With God in Hope

(Book Three, Chapters 1 to 15 of the *Ascent*)

As the intellect is purified and readied for union by faith, so the memory must undergo purification by hope and the will by charity. The treatment of the latter two faculties will be brief because, as the saint says, it is impossible not to grow in the virtues of hope and love if one is growing so profoundly in faith. The truth is that the intellect, memory, and will "depend on one another in their operations" (*AMC*, III, 1 [1]).

As far as human memory is concerned, three different objects (natural, imaginative, and spiritual) and three kinds of knowledge (natural, supernatural imaginative, and spiritual) have to be drawn into the "active night." Let us treat each of these apprehensions of memory in turn, mindful that St. John's intention in the entire *Ascent* is to help souls so disposed to advance in contemplation to union with God.

We could compare what happens to setting out on a long trip but being ludicrously overpacked. The farther you travel, the more excess baggage you have to shed because it is simply too cumbersome to carry it all. The wardrobe you thought you needed might parallel the excess "sensory means and exercises of the faculties [that] must...be left behind and in silence so that God...may effect the divine union in the soul" (*AMC*,

III, 2 [2]). Shedding unneeded luggage, packing light, you are able to move more quickly toward your destination. This detaching on the functional level, this "disencumbering, emptying, and depriving," is necessary to free the soul for travel on the transcendent plane of love. Natural operations, as St. John comments, have to be suspended to make room for "the inflow and illumination of the supernatural."

Reforming the natural capacities and capabilities of intellect, memory, and will so they do not hinder the supernatural inflow of faith, hope, and love is like a spring house cleaning of the soul. Old habits and addictions are cast out by the new broom of grace. Now fresh air can filter through your inner dwelling, unfettered by useless clutter.

One must take a risk the traveler usually avoids, namely, the risk of not knowing where precisely this journey in faith will lead. We go to God not by knowing who God is but rather through unknowing. The itinerary does not guarantee sweetness and light but includes the nights of self-denial and rejection of natural and, even in the end, of supernatural apprehensions. The memory is as subject as the other faculties are to this journey in darkness. As St. John says, "We must draw it away from its natural props and capacities and raise it above itself (above all distinct knowledge and apprehensible possession) to supreme hope in the incomprehensible God" (*AMC*, III, 2 [3]).

Natural Knowledge in the Memory

What do we remember? The soft velvet cheek of a newborn child. The first sip of cool water after cutting the grass. The fragrance of lilacs on a spring morn. The mainland outlined against the sea following a long flight home. The sound of a familiar hymn coming through the windows of an old neighborhood church. We remember, in other words, persons, places, events, and things imprinted upon our five bodily senses. While this knowledge is directly applicable to natural things, it is only analogous when applied to God.

Neither the memory nor the intellect can be united with God and at the same time cling to the distinct knowledge of God. Symbols, images, and metaphors point to God, but they cannot ever wholly comprehend God's mystery. United to God, the memory is "without form, figure, or fantasy . . . in great forgetfulness, without the remembrance of anything . . . absorbed in a supreme good" (*AMC*, III, 2 [4]).

This state of holy forgetfulness or absorption places one so much in the present, so in the here and now, that it "sweeps the fantasy of all forms and knowledge, and elevates the memory to the supernatural." St. John speaks of a "great oblivion" in which forgetfulness of memory and suspension of imagination reaches so high a degree that a long time may pass in which one is united with God yet without awareness or knowledge of what has occurred. St. Paul, for example, did not know in the course of his being caught up to "the third heaven" whether he was in the body or out of the body (cf. 2 Cor 12:1–4).

Though only God can bestow and produce these touches of union, we can enhance our receptivity to them by letting go of the naturally apprehensible forms and images we have collected in our minds about God. Paradoxically, there is a stage of forgetfulness we must go through if we are to grow more mindful of God as a mystery of love and not an object of our own mastery.

Subsequently, as we make space for grace, we may have to endure the embarrassment of being so inwardly absorbed in God that it is difficult to attend to external demands. We are "out of it" for a while, in a state of suspension where memory of details fades away in a

"cloud of forgetting," to quote the English author of the
Cloud of Unknowing. We are intent only on remembering
God, on re-membering or reuniting, so to speak, all to
the All.

It would seem that St. John is describing himself when
he admits that "this person" may forget to eat or drink,
may fail to notice if he did or left undone a certain task,
or said this or that. Since all his inner energy is concentrated on God, there is only a minimum left for "less
than God-oriented" duties and events.

It is of some consolation to know that once a person has attained the "habit of union," this relapse of
memory ceases and one more or less returns to normal. If anything, one is in possession of more energy to
attend to what has to be done in an effective and non-
distracted manner, in a way that is more supernatural or
transcendent.

Possessed by God, we can now profess God in all we
say and do. There is no split between inner inspiration
and outer incarnation, between recollection and action,
because we are one in spirit with God. Hence the operations of the memory are increasingly divinized and
transformed. We know what must be known and ignore
what must be ignored; we remember what ought to be
remembered and forget what is best forgotten; we love
what ought to be loved in God and are able to let go of
every semblance of self-seeking.

> The reason [for such expediency and efficacy] is that
> God alone moves these souls to do... works that
> are in harmony with His will and ordinance, and
> they cannot be moved toward others. Thus the works
> and prayer of these souls always produce their effect
> (*AMC*, III, 2 [10]).

This state of being and acting fully in accord with
God's will is not attained by any power of our own. It
is a pure gift of God. The most we can do is prepare

ourselves to receive it by passing through the nights of purification St. John describes during which God may effect this gift of union passively. The saint intends to discuss these matters more thoroughly in the *Dark Night* itself. In this Book of the *Ascent,* he will confine his reflections for the most part to what we are to do in response to grace's drawing us into the night. In essence, here is the advice he gives:

1. Clear the channels of memory so you can essentially remember God, that is, do not store up in your memory sensory objects, do not cling to the remembrance of things heard, seen, smelt, tasted, touched — as if they were "little gods" — but forget them all.

2. Leave your memory free to remember God by disentangling it from both earthly and heavenly considerations that are not aimed at directing you by means of retrospective disclosure to God. A good example would be the mourning process, following the death of a child. Words cannot describe how much you miss your beloved daughter or son, but at a certain point you have to let go of your tortured memories, consign her or him to God, and go on with life, remembering God's love for you and his care in life and after death for your own and all children. Thus your natural memory will not hinder but foster supernatural remembrance.

3. No matter how weary you feel while walking this road of inner reformation, never despair, for God will come to your aid at a suitable time: "It is expedient to endure and suffer patiently and with hope for so remarkable a blessing" (*AMC*, III, 2 [15]).

Obstacles on the Way to Hope

What happens if we do not purge or reform the power of memory in the way St. John proposes? He targets three definite detours that can delay our journey to God.

The first obstacle is related to two things: to the stock of worldly knowledge stored up in the chambers of our memory and to various kinds of discursive reflection that rely upon this faculty. The memory can play tricks on us. What is false seems true after enough rationalization, what is doubtful, certain. Emotions are stirred up as we return in memory to sensate objects and stimulating events. Suddenly we feel sorrowful, fearful, hateful, vain.

All these imperfections mar tranquillity of soul, resurrect old addictions, and strengthen sinful habits. Other people suffer as a result. A harsh judgment made in remembrance of things they did or left undone violates the law of love Christians are bound to obey.

As far as St. John is concerned, there is no way to overcome the thousand imperfections and trifles associated with deformed memory, with memory unpurified and unreformed by hope in God alone. Memory is like the starting button on a tape recorder. Not to turn off the tape it plays incessantly is to risk disquiet and continual "deprivation of numerous holy thoughts and considerations about God which are conducive to the reception of favors from God" (AMC, III, 3 [4]).

One risks getting caught in a never-ending cycle of old memories that stimulate habitual, addictive responses that "stick to him just as pitch to anyone who touches it." Crucial here is inner calm, not the destruction of memory but its recollection in regard to eternal and temporal things. As St. John says, there is no entry point in a recollected memory for distractions, trifles or vices. Wandering memory, by contrast, draws our meditation on a circuitous detour from whence other evils may arise. The memory, therefore, must be silenced by hope, made mute by inner stillness, so we can listen to the Spirit of God speaking in the depths of our heart. There we ought to remain, without cares or afflictions, awaiting the peace of the Lord.

St. John assures us that once we have closed the doors of intellect, memory, and will to the apprehension of both earthly and heavenly considerations, we shall be in readiness to receive the river of Christ's peace, which will fill our dried up reservoirs and "remove all the misgivings, suspicions, disturbances, and darknesses that made the soul fear it had gone astray" (*AMC*, III, 3 [6]). For the rest we should persevere in prayer and rest in the hope that divine blessings "will not be long in coming."

The demonic can also play upon the natural apprehensions of memory and profoundly distort them, adding and subtracting ideas and reasonings that move us farther from God and closer to mere human pride, avarice, anger, envy, and the other capital sins. The devil impresses false images that plague our fantasy life; Satan stimulates delusions through the ideas and discourses of memory and diminishes in the end our power to decide in favor of God.

Only by darkening memory, by closing the door tightly to this kind of diabolical harm, can we hope to be liberated for God alone. Since the devil can do nothing to us save through the operations of the inner faculties, to darken even one of them, like the memory, is to render the devil powerless (cf. *AMC*, III, 4 [1]).

Memories of sadness, for example, if clung to in an addictive manner, can create a crevice through which the demonic can slip. Thus even an appropriate response like mourning the death of a loved one can become an obstacle to hope and appreciative abandonment to our always benevolent God. St. John qualifies his counsel as follows:

> Although the good derived from this void is not as
> excellent as that arising from the application of the

soul to God, by the mere fact that it liberates us from
a lot of sorrow, affliction, and sadness — over and
above imperfections and sins — it is an exceptional
blessing (AMC, III, 4 [2]).

The final obstacle has to do with the fact that trigger
mechanisms located in the memory — for instance, a
scene of anger one replays over and over again — can
positively deprive the soul of moral and spiritual good.
Moral good "consists in the control of the passions and
the restriction of the inordinate appetites" (AMC, III, 5
[1]). The resulting peace and virtuous style of living is,
according to the saint, spiritual good. It is impossible to
attain unless we are willing to control the emotions trig-
gered by memories of these passions and the appetites
they stimulate.

In other words, thoughts awaken feelings, so it is the
process of apprehension we must learn to control. Not
so surprising is the fact that modern cognitive therapy
agrees with St. John's observation that "as often as a person begins to think about some matter, he is moved and
aroused about it according to some kind of apprehension" (AMC, II, 5 [2]). If what we think about is sad, for
instance, we will soon feel sad.

To alter the cognition is to still undergo agitation.
The best solution is not only to foster a shift from what
Adrian van Kaam calls depreciative to appreciative
thinking but also consciously to forget or completely let
go of these triggering mechanisms while lifting all things
into the light of the transcendent. There only can we experience true spiritual tranquillity. From this kernel of
spirituality there may emerge a lasting, protective shell
of morality. As St. John observes:

> An unsettled soul, which has no foundation of moral
> good, is incapable as such of receiving spiritual good.
> For this spiritual good is only impressed upon a re-
> strained and peaceful soul (AMC, III, 5 [3]).

Most importantly, if we pay too much attention to the pulls and pushes of memory, imagination, and anticipation, we will find it impossible to remain free for the unknown Mystery who is God. Hence: "The soul must go to God by not comprehending rather than by comprehending, and it must exchange the mutable and comprehensible for the Immutable and Incomprehensible" (*AMC*, III, 5 [3]).

Benefits of Forgetting for the Sake of Remembering God

When memories of this, that and the other thing spin wildly in our minds, disrupting peaceful recollection like swarms of bees swooping into a still garden, it is time again, in the words of the author of the *Cloud of Unknowing*, to press these thoughts and ideas under the "cloud of forgetting." There are many benefits that accompany this kind of discipline, the first being tranquillity and peace of soul, the absence of disturbance and willful alteration of direction. We maintain a straight course to God, remembering that "God alone suffices" (Teresa of Avila), that "purity of heart is to will one thing" (Soren Kierkegaard). Thus disposed, we are "freed from many suggestions, temptations, and movements which the devil inserts in souls through their thoughts and ideas" (*AMC*, III, 6 [2]).

Say a neighbor does something uncouth and offensive like throwing his garbage in your yard. You give him a piece of your mind, harsh words are exchanged, and both of you retreat in anger since his action turns out to be in retaliation for your children having thrown debris over his fence. The memory of this episode catches fire as you repeat what happened to your wife. She adds fuel because she never liked him or his loudmouthed ways to begin with. Soon a real feud is brewing. Any thought of working out your differences by dialogue, as neighbors ought to do, is the farthest thing from your mind. It is easy to see how the demonic can slip into this all-too-common situation. The devil plays on past memories of unresolved misunderstandings, making the exercise of Christian charity almost impossible. As St. John explains, there is one simple solution: Forget it. "When the thoughts are removed [in this case of bitterness and tension between neighbors], the devil has nothing naturally with which to wage his war on the spirit" (AMC, III, 6 [2]).

On the contrary, if both families were to make peace, forgive and forget, they would create room for the Holy Spirit and open their hearts, now closed by stubbornness and stupidity, to the Spirit's teaching. A nicer neighborhood, less friction, more friendship would be the fruit of forgetting in this sense. In fact, St. John holds that such voiding of the memory frees us from many unnecessary stresses, afflictions, and disturbances. For example, freedom from the addiction or gnawing desire for revenge is no small reward for renunciation. Worry and useless anxiety never solve problems; they only loom larger. Hence there is much wisdom in letting go. Succinctly phrased, "It is always vain to be disturbed, since being disturbed is never any help" (AMC, III, 6 [3]). Let us quote St. John's wisdom in full, for it is worth remembering, especially in agitated moments when we lose our "spiritual cool."

> Thus if the whole world were to crumble and come to an end and all things were to go wrong, it would be useless to get disturbed, for this would do more harm than good. The endurance of all with tranquil and peaceful equanimity not only reaps many blessings, but also helps the soul so that in these very adversities it may succeed in judging them and employing the proper remedy (AMC, III, 6 [3]).

This is truly the dictum of the saints: "Tranquillity of soul and peace in all things, in adversity as well as in prosperity" (*AMC*, III, 6 [4]). The key to such peace lies in releasing our memories from the grip of disturbing thoughts and ideas so that we can remember the wider vision of eternity against which temporal problems pale in importance.

Handling Memory of Supernatural Imaginative Apprehensions

Visions, locutions, revelations, spiritual sentiments — no experience that is this extraordinary can go unnoticed by the memory. Some residue at least of the religious experience imprints itself upon the mind in the guise of an image, an idea, of a remembered, somewhat ecstatic moment. We want to repeat the experience in fact, if not in fantasy, and herein resides the difficulty as St. John sees it. Such efficacious apprehensions, imprinted as they are on the memory, can encumber one's attaining "union with God in pure and integral hope" (*AMC*, III, 7 [1]).

Rather than releasing the event, rather than treating it as a real but ephemeral gift, the tendency is to recall it, often in greater and greater detail, to cling to what happened as the high point of one's spiritual life. St. John explains with some urgency that this is where people inevitably get into trouble spiritually. They end up paying too much attention to these apprehensions and not enough to the abyss of faith to which the vision or consolation points. The simple fact is that "none of the supernatural forms and ideas that can be had by the memory is God, and the soul must empty itself of all that is not God in order to go to God" (*AMC*, III, 7 [2]). Hope is no longer hope if its object is possessed. And since God cannot be possessed, only hoped in and hoped for, the soul has to be dispossessed of any substitute for God, even the highest experience of God.

If all this sounds complicated, it is simply because St. John understands our nature. Spiritually we must let go; humanly we want to cling to what we know and own. Yet only in dispossession of things, including images, forms, ideas, and memories can we hope to reach possession of God in divine union. It is like saying that only when we make room for our Divine Guest by clearing out inner clutter can God enter the room of our heart and rest there. The in-between moment may feel dry compared to what went before, but we must resist the temptation to rely too heavily on felt consolations and the sweet memories of God's presence they conjure up. Not to go beyond these delightful memories is to block the renunciation to which we are ultimately called.

Impediments to Union
With God in Hope

There are, according to St. John, five types of harm related to the memory that can hinder divine union. The first pertains to the human penchant to give a supernatural explanation to a quite natural occurrence. A priest told the story of mistaken piety in his seminary. The young man next door to him became distraught when a black spot kept appearing on his forehead, particularly in the morning and at night. Could it be a special sign of God's favor or perhaps something demonic? Others could see it and before long this "supernatural event" became the "hottest item" in the community. The delusion, it turned out, was indeed "demonic" but in the most human sense. A local practical joker had put ink in the lad's holy water font and every time he crossed himself a special sign indeed appeared!

St. John says these kinds of deception can be quantitative, that is, what is small becomes big or vice versa. Think of the proverbial "fish story." Each time the catch is recounted the sunfish takes on the proportions of a shark! Delusions that turn imaginative products into supernatural apprehensions can also be qualitative, meaning that what is darkness is defined as light. The worst instance involves the case of persons who use their piety to gain power over others deemed "less privileged" because they have not received the same supernatural communications. Charismatic religious leaders have often wielded this kind of power over gullible followers.

St. John's solution for avoiding delusion is simple: Don't attribute any importance to these rare occurrences because they are likely to be figments of an overactive religious imagination incapable of discerning what is of God and what of the devil. To be avoided assiduously are strong impressions about the good or evil of oneself or others. Only God is the judge, and it is perilous for us to risk basing our spiritual life on false premises. Hence it is wise to void our memory of these apprehensions for "they are not as great a help toward the love of God as is the least act of living faith and hope made in the emptiness and renunciation of all things" (*AMC*, III, 8 [5]).

A second harm that comes from keeping these apprehensions in the forefront of our memory has to do with the type of vanity, self-esteem, and presumption St. John targets as a grave impediment to spiritual progress. An excellent example of what he means can be found in Aldous Huxley's account of the *Devils of Loudun* where a whole convent of nuns gets caught in the mass hysteria fomented by one "visionary" whose vanity gets the best of her and through whom the demonic seduces a number of other sisters. It is as if the "visionary" relies on these supernatural wonders to give her a sense of worthiness. Pride in this sense poses as humility, and people around her are greatly confused. Some who initially resisted the hysteria are eventually swept up in the flood of confusion, mistaking, as Huxley implies, mind tricks for true mystical experience.

Matters are complicated when the "seer" tells everyone that she is unworthy to receive such favors but in the meantime harbors a hidden satisfaction that she really is someone special in God's eyes. The real source of her problem, spiritual pride, ought to be detectable when she senses in herself an aversion for anyone who does not laud her as God's instrument or who challenges her received message, or when she feels envious of another who seems to be transmitting similar communications. This is the pharisee symptom — thanking God that one is not like others and in the process despoiling what really pleases God, namely, perfect humility (cf. Lk 18:11–12). To make pious sentiments the proof of one's nearness to God, to look down on others who do not report similar feelings, is from the viewpoint of the life of the spirit sheer folly.

Two reminders may help to correct this wrong course. Virtue does not consist in having many consolations, however sublime these touches may be, but in practicing humility and taking delight in appearing to be nothing in the eyes of others. Even more to the point is the remembrance that all visions, revelations, and feelings, however sublime, are not worth a cent compared to one act of humbly executed charity. In everyday life the seeds of holiness are planted in hiddenness until God himself grants the harvest.

In describing the third harm that can come from clinging to supernatural apprehensions, St. John again stresses how vulnerable one becomes to demonic deception. It is like playing with fire. The devil presents false ideas, imaginative shapes, and efficacious suggestions to the memory under the guise of truth. He, the prince of darkness, transforms himself into an angel of light, causing the deceived soul to become desirous of these experiences and inordinately attached to the "visions" that do occur. Dazzled by what is beheld, by the sweetness of the sensation, the soul becomes blind — fascinated more by pleasure than love, fixated more on ecstatic apprehension than on the emptiness of faith. Every blunder in the spiritual or moral realm is rationalized away and one slowly but surely succumbs to the devil's seductive lies. As St. John vividly puts it: "What was wine will have turned into vinegar" (*AMC*, III, 10 [2]). The false no longer seems false, the evil no longer evil. All this — except in rare cases of true apparitions validated by church authorities over the centuries — comes from not banishing the memory of these events from one's mind from the beginning.

Two other harms may come to us if we base our spiritual beliefs on visions and other extraordinary experiences. The fourth impediment to hope relates to what the saint calls improper judgments of God. Hope, correctly understood, extends toward the unknown with utter confidence in God's revealed word. If hope is hampered by the memory of what was, it cannot soar freely toward what will be. Hence to remember this or that experience of the "beyond" as ultimate builds barriers to union. The more encumbered our memory is, the less likely we are to live in hope. This is why St. John insists that we have to "forget" self-generated images and ideas about God, for these are always *less than* God. Not to forget in this way is to risk the fifth impediment: to reduce the incomprehensible Holy to comprehensible human proportions, contrary to what our faith teaches. Memory, among other things, serves us humans as a classification system — like the memory bank of a computer. But the mystery of God escapes every attempt by human ingenuity to master it. God in his essence is infinitely *more than* any existing creature can grasp, imagine or remember. To live at one with while still longing for the transcendent is the distinctive characteristic of being human.

Benefits of Living in Hope

It remains our responsibility to relinquish or, better still, to reject the kinds of apprehensions that fire the imagination in an ecstatic manner, implant themselves in our powers of remembrance, and thereby diminish hope. St. John names five benefits associated with this purgation of mind and memory, benefits that correct the impediments already described.

Exciting as it may be to receive and recall supernatural imaginative apprehensions, it is best to restore our inner being as soon as possible to a state of spiritual rest and repose. Living from the center of faith and hope, we are freed from the trouble of having to discern which apprehensions are of God, which of the devil, and how we are to behave toward them. This releases us in turn from the drudgery and time-consuming activity of having to recount what occurred to one or a number of spiritual directors to ascertain whether an event of this sort is truly of God, self-initiated, or of demonic origin. Forgetting it absolves us from any compulsion to find the answer. Then, to address the fourth benefit, instead of wasting time engaging in a lengthy discernment process, we can find better things to do like moving our will toward God in the darkness of unknowing.

Spiritual and sensory deprivation is St. John's favored avenue to inner liberation and poverty of spirit. To hope in God without the support of interior or exterior consolations is to take a giant step in faith. Finally, we must accept the paradoxical fact that the more we *withdraw* from imaginative forms, images and figures, the more closely we *draw* to God.

As to the fear that this rule of forgetfulness might lead us to refuse God's gifts, St. John assuages it by urging us to reread Book Two, Chapters 16 and 17, of the *Ascent* where he says that any good resulting from these gifts is produced passively by no act of admission on our part. All we must do is maintain a receptive posture toward supernatural apprehensions without striving to find a natural explanation for them. It is exactly this natural or self-initiated activity that obscures the Spirit in St. John's experience.

The passive or receptive posture is essential since substantial understanding of God's call cannot be attained until the operations of the faculties cease. In a sense it is like saying that the dynamics of ego psychology must at a certain point give way to the dynamics of spirituality. As Jesus said to his disciples, "To find yourself [your true and deepest self in God] you must lose yourself [the egocentric "I" that functions as if God were an appendage of human need rather than the ground of your being]" (cf. Mk 8:34–35).

> If a person were to desire to employ his faculties actively in these supernatural apprehensions by which, as we said, he receives the spirit passively from God, he would be doing nothing less than abandoning what has been accomplished in order to redo it; neither would he be enjoying what was done, nor by his activity doing anything other than impeding God's work (*AMC*, III, 13 [4]).

In short, what God infuses the soul has to accept with no effort on its part to produce sensations or to embellish passively granted favors. If God wants to move the soul to what transcends its power and knowledge, God will do so. All that is necessary is that we watch and wait.

> This is like saying: I shall stand upon the watch of my faculties and take no step forward in my operations; thus I shall be able to contemplate what is told me: I shall understand and taste what is communicated to me supernaturally (*AMC*, III, 13 [4]).

The only action proper on our part is to enkindle the love and hope these aspirations spark in us. It is not our place to try to figure out what they signify, represent or connote. If the apprehensions come from above, they shall flow from the loving heart of God to the longing heart of the lover. If they are from below, of diabolical origin, they shall only result in dryness of spirit, in hardness of heart. "Only for the sake of moving the spirit to love should the soul at times recall the images and apprehensions which produced love" (AMC, III, 13 [6]).

To renew love, to elevate the mind to God, is a blessing to cherish, a benefit to share. A true religious experience reverberates long after the event itself and can continue to enkindle love for a lifetime. Therese of Lisieux's *Story of a Soul* or Dag Hammarskjold's *Markings* are both classic records of how the imprint of holy love can never be erased from one's heart. As often as these two believers remembered the touch of God in their life, their memories, as the diaries reveal, produced not self-aggrandizement but gratitude for the divine effects of love, undeserved yet equally unforgettable. "This is . . . a great grace, for the person upon whom God bestows it possesses . . . a mine of blessings" (AMC, III, 13 [6]).

These God-initiated glimpses can be recalled not for the sake of reproducing them by human means but to procure the effect of love, which produced them in the first place. It is most beneficial for the soul to treat the residue of what actually occurred (the figure) rather matter-of-factly so that memory does not stop at this reminder of union but flies to its source, the pure love of God known in faith, anticipated in hope, practiced in charity.

Spiritual Knowledge in the Memory

Whereas St. John is consistent in raising suspicions pertaining to corporeal and imaginative apprehensions as avenues to authentic union with God, he is favorably disposed to addressing the graced validity of God-initiated and God-oriented spiritual knowledge. Bestowed directly by God — not through any effigy or image — apprehensions of this sort are spiritually impressed on the soul; they are the object of spiritual reminiscence; the effects produced by them are sound intellectually and devotionally.

This knowledge may be related to both creatures and the Creator. In the latter case one catches directly and often spontaneously, the epiphanic depth of the cosmic, terrestrial world. To behold a scene of natural beauty — a softly murmuring mountain stream, a snow covered evergreen on Christmas Eve, a distant star on a clear, cold night — draws one who lives in hope to a deeper knowledge and love of God. The memory goes immediately to the divine source rather than stopping at any intermediary. If remembrance does not produce this effect, St. John cautions us not to desire it, for a mistake is made whenever we recall fervently the occasion of consolation and neglect to remember first and foremost the God who consoles.

As often as we meditate upon the Creator, wellspring of every good and perfect gift, we can be sure spiritual knowledge from whatever source it is derived (from Bible study, from reading the classics, from actual experience) will produce a notable effect — that of leading us to a life of faith, hope, and love. To receive and thank God for these touches of divine self-communication becomes not an occasional point of wonder but a mode of unceasing prayer. We begin to taste the power of transforming love, to glimpse the goal of union with God. This ongoing reminiscence does not depend on our conjuring forth from memory any particular form, image or figure but on a felt sense of being, here and now, in the presence of the living God, of enjoying the effects of ongoing spiritual renewal.

St. John concludes his discussion of this portion of the "active night" by recommending a general rule of conduct that ought to guide true seekers. We shall summarize his advice by again using the imperative tense. He frames his counsel by reminding the reader that the aim of this "night" is to help us reach the goal of union with God in the memory. His reasoning goes like this:

> The object of hope is something unpossessed; the less other objects are possessed, the more capacity and ability there is to hope for this one object, and consequently the more hope; the greater the possessions, the less capacity and ability for hope, and consequently so much less of hope; accordingly, in the measure that a person dispossess his memory of forms and objects, which are not God, he will fix it upon God and preserve it empty, in the hope that God will fill it (AMC, III, 15 [1]).

What, then, must one do to live in perfect hope?

1. As often as distinct ideas, forms, and images occur to you, immediately, without resting in them, turn to God with loving affection, empty of everything rememberable.

2. Do not think or look upon these things for a longer time than is sufficient for doing what you have to do, especially if the memories refer to any specific duty or responsibility.

3. Consider what passes through your mind without becoming attached to any of it, without seeking gratification from it, lest these ideas — not God — clasp tight tentacles onto your soul.

St. John adds that he is not against images as such nor opposed to venerating relics and like reminders of the Holy. He wants only to be sure we understand the

difference between the "painted" and the "living" image
(cf. *AMC*, III, 15 [2]). All such memorial devices must be
used as means to an end and not the other way around.
The problem compounds when the images are linked
to so-called supernatural visions, for there the danger
of delusion is obvious from all that the saint has said.
What is of profit to us is the evocation by means of an
image like the statue of a saint of the love we feel for
whomever is represented. Images and the memory of
them need not hinder but may actually help us advance
on one condition — that we do not pay more attention
to them than is necessary. When God bestows a special grace upon us, we must be ready "to soar . . . from
the painted image to the living God" (*AMC*, III, 15 [2]).
Now is the time to live in forgetfulness of anything created or of anything pertaining to the created so that we
can remember only God, a memory St. John winsomely
captures in the last stanza of his "dark night":

> I abandoned and forgot myself,
> Laying my face on my Beloved;
> All things ceased; I went out from myself,
> Leaving my cares
> Forgotten among the lilies.
>
> (*The Dark Night*)

8

Purification of the Will by Love

(Book Three, Chapters 16 and 17 of the *Ascent*)

In the remaining chapters of the *Ascent*, St. John names four emotions of the will, joy, hope, sorrow, and fear. Because the text ends abruptly, he is able to offer only an extensive analysis of joy. The "joy" of which he speaks is not comparable to the peace of God that passes understanding. It is not transcendent joy but a form of gratification or pleasure associated with bodily needs, or at most a kind of functional satisfaction associated with worldly accomplishments. Neither "joys" can quiet the soul's quest for the highest, lasting joy of union with God.

The other affects of the heart, while not treated in detail, connote similar meanings. By "hope" St. John refers to egocentric expectations. Even if they do come true, they do not make us happy. "Sorrow" is a depreciative attitude, a source of depression and despair. It results also when we make anything less than God an ultimate concern. "Fear" suggests useless, rambling worry, anxiety, and a lack of confidence in God. It breeds persistent insecurity, a sure sign that we trust ourselves more than God.

Proper Direction of the Will

St. John's initial considerations of the "active night of the will" disclose a formula for happiness based on the Great Commandment — to love God with our whole heart, mind and will, and to love others as we love ourselves. The strength of the soul, its faculties, passions, and appetites, is rooted decisively in the will, the locus of human freedom. Whenever we opt by the power of our will to turn away from God toward that which is less than God we suffer the consequences: disharmony, disintegration, and death spiritually, if not physically, speaking. Directed toward God, mind and heart, desires and dreams, wants and needs take on a new, transcendent meaning. We love all in God, we do what has to be done for God, we wait upon God in prudence, perseverance, and peace.

In a letter written to a Discalced Carmelite friar, dated Segovia, April 14, 1589, St. John recalls why it is that we must purge our will of inordinate attachments to and feelings for any persons, events or things that have become God-substitutes for us. They simply cannot live up to their promise of fulfillment. Nothing on this earth can be anything but a pointer to the "More Than." He writes:

> Thus it is obvious that none of all those particular things in which it can rejoice is God. In order to be united with Him, the will must consequently be emptied of and detached from all disordered appetite and satisfaction in every particular thing in which it can rejoice whether earthly or heavenly, temporal or spiritual, so that purged and cleansed of all inordinate satisfactions, joys, and appetites it might be wholly occupied in loving God with its affections. For if in any way the will can comprehend God and be united with Him, it is through love, and not through any gratification of the appetite (*Minor Works*, Letter 12).

This radical renunciation of *all* for the sake of the *All* is the only legitimate avenue to inner and outer liberation. Once we pass through this midnight moment of relinquishing desires and move with grace toward a new dawning of freedom, we begin to love all in God and to see God in all. Everything is given back to us but on a new plane of spirituality. That is why the same saint who preached renunciation can celebrate in ecstasy his place in creation.

> Mine are the heavens and mine is the earth. Mine are the nations, the just are mine, and mine the sinners. The angels are mine, and the Mother of God, and all things are mine; and God Himself is mine and for me, because Christ is mine and all for me (*Sayings of Light and Love*, "Prayer of a Soul Taken with Love").

Unruly Affections of the Will

The emotions sidetracking the soul from this wider vision are, as already named, *joy* (gratification in "little beyonds"); *hope* (expectation of fulfillment on this earth); *sorrow* (sadness when no-thing satisfies); and *fear* (anxious avoidance of any risk, especially the leap of faith into the arms of a transcendent-immanent, wholly beyond yet unashamedly near God).

The aim of purging the will of these unruly affections is to enable the soul to find itself in God, to fly so high that one can at least "catch the tail" of the (divine) prey. As the poem which provides the title for this book suggests:

> When I ascended higher
> My vision was dazzled,
> And the most difficult conquest
> Was achieved in darkness;
> But since I was seeking love
> The leap I made was blind and dark

And I rose so high, so high,
That I took the prey.
(*More Stanzas Applied to
Spiritual Things*)

Affections and emotions are not problems in themselves. Feelings are feelings. It is the thought behind
them that has to be transformed. Once the intellect is
purified by faith and the memory by hope, then the
will in response to love chooses rightly. Similarly *joy* (in
God's goodness), *hope* (in God's promise), *sorrow* (for
our blindness), and *fear* (understood as awe and wonder) become aids, not obstacles, to oneness with God.

In this sense the union of likeness lost by original and
actual sin can begin to be recovered. We are "like" the
one in whose image we have been made when we rejoice
only in what is for God's honor and glory, when we
hope for nothing else, when we feel sorrow only about
what deflects us from our goal, when we reverence God
so much that perfect love casts out fear (cf. 1 Jn 4:18).
Surrender to God's will gives us peace and a sense of
purpose. Work is effective service devoted to God's reign
on earth. Prayer is an inner atmosphere of unceasing
adoration. As the popular hymn suggests, where love
and charity abide, there God is ever found.

The converse is equally true: When these emotions
are unbridled, when the will guiding them is not itself
guided by God, they are, to quote St. John, the source
of all vices and imperfections. As one goes, so goes the
other. In other words:

> The less strongly the will is fixed on God, and the
> more dependent it is upon creatures, the more these
> four passions combat the soul and reign in it. It then
> very easily finds joy in what deserves no rejoicing,
> and hope in what brings it no profit, and sorrow over
> what should perhaps cause rejoicing, and fear where
> there is no reason for fear (*AMC*, III, 16 [4]).

As long as these passions hold a soul prisoner, one can neither experience equanimity nor grow in wisdom.

Joy and Its Objects: An Exercise in Inner Purification

According to St. John, we will or choose only what satisfies us, what gives us pleasure or, for his purposes, joy. For example, we decide to stop at an ice cream parlor instead of going straight home because we know how pleasurable it will be to have a cone on a hot summer day. We muster the will power to persevere through summer school because we know how satisfying it will be to graduate someday. By the same token, we decide not to eat a certain food that upsets us, no matter how good it tastes, because there is no pleasure involved in being sick. We will not to follow our parents' plans for what we ought to be because they no longer match what we have come to know about ourselves.

The point St. John is trying to make is that "joy" is satisfaction felt when we attain the object our will desires or considers fitting to produce pleasure. On the spiritual plane, he suggests a distinction between active joy, when we understand the object or cause of this feeling, and passive joy when we find ourselves rejoicing inwardly but without any clear and distinct understanding of why we feel this way. If we are hungry and then eat, it's no mystery why we are happy. If we are fasting and have nothing to eat and still feel joy, then the cause remains veiled in mystery. This joy is a gift. We do not possess it; it possesses us.

St. John lists the six main objects of active and voluntary joy, relating each to what we physically, emotionally, functionally, and spiritually would call "good." These are: *temporal, natural, sensory, moral, supernatural,* and *spiritual.* By discussing each of these joy-evoking

sources in turn, he hopes to sharpen our ability to reg-
ulate our choices according to reason versus instinctive
movements of aversion and attraction. He wants us to respond, not to react, for only when we exercise response-
ability can we concentrate the vigor of our sense-ability
upon the source, the radical root, of all joy: our gracious
and merciful God. Hence, in principle, the will should
rejoice only in what is for the honor and glory of God.
What gives God the greatest honor is our willingness to
serve him in obedience, poverty of spirit, and respectful
love (cf. *AMC*, III, 17 [2]). This threefold path of spiritual deepening is thus the right choice for anyone whose
goal is union with God.

9

The Passion of Joy

(Book Three, Chapters 18 to 32 of the *Ascent*)

Joy in Temporal Goods

Were commercial advertising the main source of truth, we might conclude that "temporal goods" are the guarantors of earthly happiness. We would envy the rich and famous, seek the status of the *Fortune* 500, compete madly for top positions, direct our entire reservoir of energy toward being a dignitary. Were we to read only romantic novels about the family, we would soon come to believe that the best life has to offer is a good marriage, two children, money in the bank, and nice in-laws — period!

The world of advertising and public relations focuses our attention on the temporal, on the here and now possibility of total gratification. In themselves these earthly blessings are not a hindrance to transcendent openness. What obscures the eternal is our tendency to absolutize or make ultimate and *lasting* the importance of things and people that are by their nature *passing*. These "givens" are meant to be avenues, not obstacles, to true joy. Only if God is seen as their origin and only if God is served through them can we escape the pitfall of addiction, the sin of idolatry.

Harms Due to Attachment. St. John identifies the main harm associated with inordinate attachment to temporal

goods as "withdrawal from God" (cf. *AMC*, III, 19–20).
How right he is! Do we not live in an era where God,
instead of being at the center of our lives, is relegated
to the periphery or forgotten altogether. For many the
Sabbath has become a symptom of "forgetfulness of the
Sacred." Sunday is no longer a day of rest but a day
to shop. In other words, excessive addiction to "having"
inflicts "privative" harm on our spiritual formation powers insofar as it literally deprives us of our nearness to
God. Yet this transcendent potency alone renders us, in
the words of Adrian van Kaam, "distinctively human."
Therefore, to quote St. John: "Just as every good is due
to an approach toward God through the affection of the
will, so withdrawal from Him through creature affection breeds every harm and evil in the soul" (*AMC*, III,
19 [1]).

Once this deprivation occurs, four additional degrees
of "positive" harm may be set in motion. First of all,
St. John alerts us to the phenomena of "surfeit" and
"backsliding." Curiously the more we engulf ourselves
in the single-minded, single-willed pursuit of happiness
through amassing temporal things, the less room there is
in our inner life for God. Ironically, this surfeit is never
satisfying. We always need the next thing or the new relationship. All the while we "backslide," moving closer
to temporal goods but farther from the one Good that
quenches our insatiable desire. Addictions of any sort
blunt the mind in relation to God, obscure right judgment, and dull our sensitivity to what alone can fulfill
us: a personal turning to God, our maker and redeemer
(cf. Dt 32:15).

The second positive harm is vividly described by
St. John as spiritual gluttony. Figuratively, if not literally, it makes us "grow fat and spread out" (cf. *AMC*, III,
19 [5]). The will to seek God in purity of heart and poverty of spirit dissipates. One loses the discipline of doing

spiritual exercises and searches frantically for worldly
things. The life of the spirit grows lukewarm. Before
long one may compromise virtue, act unethically, and
grow callous to those in need. If one goes to church at
all, it may be a mere formality done out of a sense of
duty, not love.

Soon, if the addiction persists, a person risks complete abandonment of God. The sin of covetousness commands the will. A criminal boss, for instance, is so
engrossed in drug trafficking that he cares nothing about
God's commands. He is a man of this world only, a
friend of darkness, greedy, anxious that other thugs will
steal his territory or snuff him out, never satisfied with
what he has collected, always wanting more.

The end result of this process is obvious: complete
departure from God, almost irreversible addiction to
avarice. Money becomes god for such a person. To gain it
is everything; to lose it drives one to despair and death.
Utterly lost souls commit suicide, as happened in the
Great Depression when bankers jumped out of office
buildings because they could not suffer the temporal
loss, demonstrating "with their own hands the miser-
able reward that comes from such a god" (*AMC*, III, 19
[10]). Death, not life, idolatry, not worship, is the result
of making anything less than God or for the service of
God the sole source of our joy.

> Many, today, in various ways belong to the category
> of this fourth degree. Out there in the world, their rea-
> son darkened through covetousness in spiritual mat-
> ters, they serve money and not God, and they are
> motivated by money rather than by God, and they
> give first consideration to the temporal price and not
> to the divine value and reward. In countless ways
> they make money their principal god and goal and
> give it precedence to God, their ultimate end (*AMC*,
> III, 19 [9]).

Benefits of Detachment. To counterpoint this sad, un-happy picture of an attached heart, St. John rehearses firmly and gently the benefits of formative detachment. This means, in effect, saying "no" for the sake of a greater "yes." As we train ourselves to recognize and relinquish small attachments, we will not have to fear becoming addicted to idols as earlier depicted.

The first step toward freedom of spirit is vigilance of heart. We need to be alert to any source of gratification that becomes a preoccupation of the will ("I must have it to be happy"). These "musts" need to be subjected immediately to the cognitive powers of the intellect, to a process of clear reasoning ("Why am I so intense about this desire? Is it true that having such-and-such or doing this or that would make me totally happy? And what about God in all of this? What is God's will for me?").

Reason can bring sober clarity to a sometimes frivo-lous and impulsive or compulsive will. A wise use of imagination may also help to cure the pang of inordi-nate desire as this story from the wisdom of the desert humorously illustrates:

> Abba Olympios of the Cells was tempted to fornica-tion. His thoughts said to him, "Go, and take a wife." He got up, found some mud, made a woman and said to himself, "Here is your wife, now you must work hard in order to feed her." So he worked, giving himself a great deal of trouble. The next day, making some mud again, he formed it into a girl and said to his thoughts, "Your wife has had a child, you must work harder so as to be able to feed her and clothe your child." So, he wore himself out doing this, and said to his thoughts, "I cannot bear this weariness any longer." They answered, "If you cannot bear such weariness, stop wanting a wife." God, seeing his ef-forts, took away the conflict from him and he was at peace (*The Sayings of the Desert Fathers*, trans. Benedicta Ward [Kalamazoo, MI: Cistercian Publications, 1975]).

Through this process of cognitive reasoning and imaginative variation, the monk moved from a state of being imprisoned by his desires to a feeling of profound relief and release. In this case the cessation of excessive attachment to a fantasy led to the initiation of spiritual rest and tranquillity and the complementary benefit of peaceful confidence in God (cf. *AMC*, III, 20 [2]).

Withdrawing from temporal goods as the cause of entanglement of soul also enhances worshipful presence to the things of God in creation. We are less inclined to use or abuse things for the benefit of personal or economic gain. We may even develop an ecological sensitivity, an epiphanic ability to see creatures in God and God in creatures. As a painting looks beautiful when we stand back and view it from a distance, so we obtain more joy in things when we let go of possessiveness and live in dispossession of them. This reverential attitude enables us to see into the substance of the thing, its epiphanic depth, rather than to be attentive only to its temporal attributes. By passing beyond the need for instantaneous gratification or mercenary ownership, we can experience true transcendent joy. Every time we break away from the bonds of vanity and concern for our own consolation, we liberate our heart for the service of God.

Joy in Natural Goods

By no merit of our own, simply by virtue of congenital forces guided by the forming hand of God, we may be endowed with beauty, grace, and elegance. St. Teresa of Avila certainly had all three attributes. From the record of her accomplishments, we can assume that despite the headaches and stomach pains she herself admits, she had a basically sound psyche, a strong constitution, a good mind. Her writings reveal a woman of keen intelligence, superb discretion, and excellent talents in reasoning and experiential analysis. But she also knew how quickly vanity could impel her away from her only viable opening to God: the virtue of humility. For her to have rejoiced or taken pride in these natural gifts without giving thanks to God would distort God's intention in giving them: that through her the Good News of God's glory might be better known, loved, and served.

Vain presumption and inordinate attachment twist the very graces and favors meant to honor God into occasions that give offense to God. A sick piety, emerging from repressed masochistic tendencies, might incline one to find the solution to vanity in self-inflicted disfigurement. Odd practices like flagellation and the wearing of hair shirts and chastity belts were running rampant at the time St. John was writing.

Such neurotic excesses were in many cases disguised forms of pride, the opposite of prudence and temperance. The way to purification of will is to forego vain pleasure (captured in the image of standing before the mirror admiring oneself from morning to night) by remembering that these natural endowments of body and mind rise from the earth and return to it; they are here today and gone tomorrow. Only the beauty of God shining forth in the inmost core of our being flashes its light into our spirit in time and lasts for eternity.

Harms Due to Attachment. To further this analysis, St. John outlines a number of harms resulting from inordinate attachment to natural goods (cf. *AMC*, III, [22]). Unquestionably, the obstacles of pride and vainglory head the list, puffing one up with presumption and an air of looking down upon or disesteeming "other poor devils who don't look as great as I, have as much money to spend," and so on. The senses in such a scenario are incited to sensual delights, for example, lust without love, because conscience is covered over by the quest for pleasure and the complacency this breeds. As St. John says:

> The extent and enormity of the disaster arising from joy in natural graces and beauty is patent, since on account of this joy we hear everyday of many murders, lost reputations, insults, squandered fortunes, rivalries, quarrels, and of so many adulteries, rapes, and fornications, and of fallen saints so numerous that they are compared to the third part of the stars of heaven cast down to earth by the tail of the serpent (Rv 12:4) (*AMC*, III, 22 [3]).

This tragic self-deception deepens when one becomes the ready recipient of flattery. The proverbial cocktail party replete with cliches and competition for attention comes to mind. At such moments reason and judgment are as dull as unsharpened blades. Moral values cannot easily pierce through the pleasure principle. The transcendence dynamic becomes tepid; the life of the spirit grows lukewarm; vital gratification becomes one's preferred goal. Immersed in creaturely concerns, one has no time to think of a loving Creator. All things spiritual appear tedious. God, who alone is immutable, gradually fades from view.

Benefits of Detachment. Against the backdrop of this analysis of spiritual death, we can better appreciate the benefits derived from not taking vain pleasure in natural goods but making our norm of joy whether or not we are serving God. This standard has many other benefits. Besides causing us to love God and pursue the good, it fosters the foundational dispositions of humility and charity. One small gesture of self-denial reaps a bounty of blessings, including tranquillity of soul, diminishment of distractions, recollection, and purity of mind and body.

A virtue seldom mentioned in our day but remembered by St. John is modesty of the eyes. In a neon-flashing, looks-conscious culture, where everything from low level pornography to classy portraiture is available for visual consumption, this virtue is refreshing to read about. "By guarding the senses, the gates of the soul, one decidedly safeguards and brings increase to one's peace and purity of soul" (*AMC*, III, 23 [3]).

St. John knows that what enters the imagination and memory through sight can be a source of great temptation. Hence freedom from "obscene objects and ideas" (*AMC*, III, 23 [4]) frees the soul for a rational and spiritual love of self and others in God, with the respect and gentility implied in this commitment. Too much attention to natural goods sets one up for eventual disappointment because these endowments will end someday. Countless other vanities, especially the need to please others at the expense of being pleasing to God, begin to count less and less until one reaches the goal of renunciation, that is, liberation of spirit "by which the soul easily conquers temptations, passes through trials, and grows prosperously in virtue" (*AMC*, III, 23 [6]).

Joy in Sensory Goods

The senses, so to speak, are access routes for receiving pleasure or again, to use St. John's term, joy. "Goods" abound pertinent to these senses. We see light, hear music, smell flowers, taste coffee, touch feathers. Certain objects send our imagination soaring, prompt a thousand memories, stimulate longings for a time when these goods might come together in a moment of sheer joy. It is easy for us to stay absorbed in them and miss the transcendent truth toward which they are pointing. The senses cannot give us knowledge of God as God. To expect to find total gratification in this sensate sphere is a hindrance to further progress. We have to be especially careful that prayer and devotion are not a pretext for merely feeling pious but a response, even in aridity, to God's loving call.

> Though the intention of these persons is directed to God, the effect they receive is recreation of the senses,

from which they obtain weakness and imperfection
more than the quickening of their will and its surrender to God (AMC, III, 24 [4]).

St. John proposes a test of maturity in the life of the
spirit by saying in so many words: If you see something
pleasing or taste something good, or whatever the sense
stimulation might entail, and you spontaneously pass
through and beyond what is presented to the praise of
God, you are growing spiritually. The affection of your
will does not rest on this or that gift but goes to the
heart of the Divine Giver. The senses then serve the
purpose for which God gave them to us, namely, that
through them we might come to know, love, and serve
our Maker. The appetite for sensory gratification as such
gives way to a general loving attention to God, so nour-
ishing to our spirit that we have no need for anything
else. Such freedom from the clutch of "little joys" endows the soul with the grace of lasting transcendent joy
in union with God.

Harms Due to Attachment. Numerous harms hold the
soul back like barnacles on a ship if sensory detachment
does not occur. Significantly, the types of harm associated with the other kinds of joy have their source in this
one. To seek and attain pleasure in what is visible to
the eye, as if this were ultimate, is to evoke vanity of
spirit, mental distractions, impurity in thoughts, envy,
and jealousy. Composure of soul becomes a rare com-
modity as one is hounded by the wolf of covetousness.
What we see, we want. In contemporary parlance, what
is presented to our sight for consumption, we rush to
consume — and God's will is hardly our concern.

Similarly, to attend inordinately to pleasures derived
from hearing can result in the bad habits of gossip, impulsive judgment of others, wandering thoughts, as if
one's ears were a sonar system responding to beeps, and

wild forays of the imagination based on the paltry evidence of hearsay or the ever elusive "they."

Oversensitivity to the need to surround oneself with only pleasant smells would probably mean the closing of hundreds of hospitals and mission stations. This appetite unchecked could arouse in one a disgust for the poor, as when aristocrats tour hovels with perfumed handkerchiefs, feeling aversion for the serving class and all who in any way "smell bad." Christian charity is thus replaced by spiritual irresponsiveness and unsubmissiveness of heart in humble things. Perhaps we can understand why it was so important for a fastidious youth like St. Francis of Assisi to kiss a leper.

Abusing the sense of taste leads obviously to the sins of gluttony, drunkenness, and general discord. One can see the effect of this abuse in alcoholic families where children grow up in fear and anger, with false guilt feelings and withdrawal symptoms. Such abuse also incites lust, for, as studies show, alcoholism and incest are not an uncommon combination.

Besides bodily sickness, this attachment to taste can cause a kind of spiritual torpor — think of a stuffed lion lying dazed in the sun — and a resulting tepidity, distracting to the other senses and linked in general with vital and functional discontent. The only thing to which an addict who will not acknowledge his or her disease is committed is the source of the next "fix." To taste that "high," even to pay the price of coming down and needing more of the substance to overcome tolerance, is the only thing that matters. At a time when one needs God more than ever, one settles for a passing substitute that only tastes good.

Addiction to touch may incite lust and license of tongue. This same appetite, in St. John's analysis, engenders cowardice, cringing fear, incipience, and the futile search for a warm womb of security where one will be petted and pampered and never told to persevere. The needy one is inconstant, confused, unresponsive to the call of conscience, as he or she drifts from one "this-is-it" relationship to the next, neither knowing how to take counsel or to give it, seemingly devoid of an ability to reason, awash in a sway of will-less emotions.

In all of these cases, spiritual exercises, if these ever were practiced, are slim to nonexistent and a generally lackadaisical attitude draws one away from the sacraments of reconciliation and the eucharist.

Benefits of Detachment. By contrast, one who lives in the right rhythm of formative attachment and detachment in relation to sensory goods enjoys many benefits on all levels of his or her being, from health-related issues to the heights of contemplative prayer. Freed from the distractions caused by excessive use of the senses, recollected in God, one can grow in virtue and advance toward the union of likeness. Physical, emotional, and rational needs and desires serve the transcendent longing for God; they are never severed from it.

Whereas taking pleasure in sensory goods for their own sake leads to a hundredfold distress, lifting all these goods to God results in a hundredfold deepening of spirituality. Joy finds its true object. Anything sacred or secular presented to the senses is immediately re-presented to God. There is thus no split between seeing and believing; hearing is praising and so on with the other senses. "Consequently, this person, now of pure heart, finds in all things a joyful, pleasant, chaste, pure, spiritual, glad, and loving knowledge of God" (*AMC*, III, 26 [6]). From the point of view of eternal life, St. John offers the assurance that "there will be an increase of essential glory in the soul that responds to the love of God and denies sensible goods for Him" (*AMC*, III, 26 [8]). He quotes 2 Corinthians 4:17, noting with St. Paul that for every

momentary and perishable joy a person denies there will
be worked in him or her an eternal weight of glory.

Joy in Moral Goods

It is difficult at first to grasp why St. John would raise
the issue of one's being joyful about the exercise of the
virtues, the practice of works of mercy, the observance
of God's law, and the expression of cordiality and kind-
ness. It is precisely when one is approaching the inner
chambers of goodness that one risks growing compla-
cent. To put the problem bluntly, one is in danger of
being proud about being humble! It is possible to feel
so good about being good that one forgets that he or
she is but an instrument, a servant of the Most High, a
messenger of the mystery.

These works rightly bring with them the rewards of
peace and tranquillity, a right and ordered use of reason,
actions resulting from mature deliberation (cf. *AMC*, III,
27 [2]). No nobler possessions can be known on earth —
on one condition. We must perform these works for the
honor and glory of God, and for no other gain. A good
example is given by St. John:

> For the sake of directing his joy in moral goods to God,
> the Christian should keep in mind that the value of his
> good works, fasts, alms, penances, etc., is not based
> upon their quantity and quality so much as upon the
> love of God practiced in them, and that consequently
> they are deeper in quality the purer and more en-
> tire the love of God is by which they are performed,
> and the less self-interest there is concerning earthly or
> heavenly joy, pleasure, comfort, and praise (*AMC*, III,
> 27 [5]).

Harms Due to Attachment. Lacking this motivation, we
risk, according to St. John, a slew of consequent harms.
The first of these is vanity, an old enemy of the pilgrim
soul, starkly described in Ecclesiastes 2:10–11:

> I denied my eyes nothing that they desired, refused
> my heart no pleasure, for I found all my hard work a
> pleasure, such was the return for all my efforts. I then
> reflected on all that my hands had achieved and all
> the effort I had put into its achieving. What futility it
> all was, what chasing after the wind! There is nothing
> to be gained under the sun.

Because such accomplishments are also spiritual in nature, their perversion by pride can be particularly perni-
cious, leading from vainglory and presumption to public
boasting.

Following upon the heels of self-complacency is the
tendency to judge others as less righteous, as downright
imperfect, and in true pharisaic fashion to feel contempt.
Soon one ceases to perform works that do not bring personal gratification and the chance of outside praise. People perpetuate in memorial tombs "their name, lineage,
or nobility" (*AMC*, III, 28 [5]). One calculates when to
look pious, when to smile at superiors, when to appear
in the chapel and where to sit to be noticed. It is as if
they adore themselves more than God. Such piety does
not find its reward in God but in worldly honor.

> Some want praise for their works; others, thanks; oth-
> ers talk about them and are pleased if this person or
> that or even the whole world knows about them; at
> times they want their alms, or whatever they are do-
> ing, to pass through the hands of another that it may
> be better known; others desire all these aspects to-
> gether (*AMC*, III, 28 [5]).

The only way to avoid the harm of sounding one's
trumpet (cf. Mt 6:2), says St. John, and to prevent things
from going from bad to worse is to hide one's work
so that only God might see it, not even desiring that
anyone pay attention to our accomplishments. Even so, it
is necessary to go one step further: "[One] should desire
neither the complacency of esteeming his work as if it

had value. . . " (*AMC*, III, 28 [6]). As scripture puts it,
our left hand ought not to know what our right hand is
doing (cf. Mt 6:3).

When one fails to advance in perfection because one
fails to advance in humility, it is easy to grow discour-
aged and backslide. Lost is the spirit of perseverance.
Replacing it is the delusion that doubling up on spiritual exercises will increase satisfaction. Instead one only
feels more aridity. Motivated by self-seeking rather than
by self-denial, one misses the mark of real advancement,
stubbornly refusing to take counsel and reasonable instruction from one wiser than he or she. It is hard to admit that what seems so right has proven to be so wrong.
Moral deeds have been done, but for the motive of increasing joy in oneself, not submission to God. Hardly
anyone escapes this danger. Before long this "outstand-
ing citizen," this "pillar of the church," this "mirror of
virtue" grows slack in love of God and charity to others and may even fall into the corruption he or she so
publicly abhorred.

Benefits of Detachment. A new depth of conversion is
required if the soul is to be freed from temptations and
boastfulness of heart. What has to change is the whimsi-
cal inclination to do good works when one feels like it or
to make resolutions with no intention of keeping them,
starting and stopping projects but never completing any
of them. St. John recommends that we restore diligence
and apply the promise of precise accomplishment to our
endeavors. We must base what has to be done not on the
satisfaction or lack thereof we may receive. For too many
when work ceases to satisfy, it ceases, period. If feeling
good is our goal, the work will go down the drain when
our mood shifts. Thus to withdraw our will from personal satisfaction as such and to attach it to what has to
be done for God is the key to success in a spiritual sense.

There is, moreover, a divine benefit to all of this: By
virtue of our willingness to subdue vain joy, we grow
in poverty of spirit, in meekness, humility, and prudence. One acts "neither impetuously and hastily, compelled by . . . irascible joy; nor presumptuously, affected
by . . . esteem for the work due to the joy it gives; nor
incautiously, blinded by joy" (*AMC*, III, 29 [4]). A right
balance of work and prayer comes into play. Who one
is, what one does, is pleasing to God and others, for who
would not be pleased by a worker who is freed of anger,
avarice, gluttony, sloth, and envy?

Joy in Supernatural Goods

Until now we have been reflecting with St. John on
natural endowments given to us by God that can
return the glory to God or become excuses for self-
aggrandizement. St. John proceeds to apply the same
criteria of appraisal to gifts and graces of God that
exceed our natural faculties and powers, such as wisdom, knowledge and faith healing, performing miracles,
prophesying, and discerning spirits, interpreting words
and speaking in tongues. God, he says, bestows these
gifts solely for the profit of others, not to "puff up"
the recipient.

Two benefits are to be found in regard to these supernatural goods. One is temporal for indeed, as the gospel
tells us, the sick are cured, sight is restored to the blind,
the dead are raised, demons expelled, the future fore-
told (cf. Mt 11:4–5). These gifts belonging to Jesus were
given to the apostles in the early church and to people
chosen by God up to our day. However efficacious these
works may be, they are in St. John's opinion of little or
no importance if the second benefit is not present. This
essential factor is spiritual, that is to say, an increase in

the knowledge and love of God evoked by these works in the one who performs them and in those for whom they are accomplished (cf. *AMC*, III, 30 [5]).

In and by themselves, miraculous events are not the means of uniting the soul to God. The more they are focused on as the source of union rather than as a call to deeper faith, the more they ought to be treated with suspicion. According to St. John and other church authorities over the ages, they can be distorted by the devil (cf. 1 Cor 13:1–2 and Mt 7:22–23). After all, "What profit is there in anything that is not the love of God, and what value has it in His sight?" (*AMC*, III, 30 [5]).

Harms Due to Attachment. The harms associated with supernatural goods have basically to do with our not centering our joy solely on the fulfillment of God's will. In a word, the first pitfall is deception. Actively, it is easy to impress oneself and others by such astounding accomplishments and to rejoice in them. But deception soon occurs. It becomes difficult under a blanket of praise and popularity to discern true from false spirits. To know how and at what time to exercise these gifts calls for prayer, wise counsel, and inner light. Unfortunately one may be so caught up in esteem for these "miracles" in themselves that there is no time for appraisal.

Deception also erodes good judgment. One becomes at inappropriate times and in strange places a performer, a miracle worker, as if one can program the pace of grace in accordance with the demands of the crowd. Such attempts open one passively to perversion by the devil as in the case of "wizards, enchanters...and witches" (*AMC*, III, 31 [5]).

> It should be noted that all those magicians and soothsayers who lived among the children of Israel and were expelled from the land of Saul had fallen into so

many abominations and delusions because of their desire to imitate the genuine prophets (*AMC*, III, 31 [6]).

It is vitally important, adds St. John, not to rejoice either in the supernatural gift in question or its use and
to wait at all times upon the action of grace. "God,
who grants the grace supernaturally for the utility of the
Church or its members, will...move [one] supernaturally as to the manner and time in which [one] should
use it" (*AMC*, III, 31 [7]).

Because these gifts attract so much attention to a
healer, for example, they can be detrimental to faith, especially if one starts to rely too heavily on the "seen"
as tangible proof of God's power. Perhaps without in-
tending to do so a twofold deterrent occurs. In regard
to others, to use such gifts outside the time ordained
by God and without necessity can engender in already
weak people further distrust when they do not produce
expected results, and a contempt for strong faith — faith
in darkness — when they do. In regard to the gifted individual, he or she is in danger of paying too much
attention to these miracles and of losing in the process
the substantial habit of faith in the face of a mystery that
always remains obscure.

St. John believes, as do many, that where signs and
testimonies abound, there is less merit in believing because God works these marvels when faith is weak and
when it becomes more important to *see* extraordinary
events than to *hear* the word of God. As Jesus said to
Thomas, the Doubter, blessed are those who do not see
yet still believe (cf. Jn 20:25–29). Signs and wonders occur, it would seem, in the babyhood of the spiritual life,
not so much when one matures (cf. *AMC*, III, 31 [8]).

The last of these harms, as we might guess by now, is
vainglory. When a person takes pride in these phenomena, like a faith-healer who craves the attention of the

media, he or she soon falls into vanity and becomes an easy target for demonic seduction.

Benefits of Detachment. Were St. John alive today, he would see as many benefits associated with our saying "no" to the enjoyment of supernatural goods as he did in his time. As the saying goes, if we play with fire, we are likely to get burnt — and in the realm of spirituality there are many explosive charges. People perform healings that may be the result of purely natural forces. They hear voices from the "other side." Witches and so-called "new age spiritualists" claim to be "channels" for ancient deities. Gullible believers put their faith in the power of "crystals," in astrological charts and fortune-telling cards, claiming to provide access to the occult. In such a climate of the fantastic it is more urgent than ever to heed St. John's sagacious advice to negate, annihilate, deny, and dismiss any gratification we may feel for such "supernatural" feats.

The benefits of doing so are that we withdraw the joy of our will from all that is not God and concentrate our whole mind and heart on praising and extolling God alone. In faith we come to know God as God; we listen to the words of scripture that tell us who God is; we apply our will to loving God alone and not relying so much on disclosures of marvelous deeds. The more our faith and service are offered to God freed from dependency on signs and testimonies, the more we may be extolled by God when we least expect it. It is not that we deny the truths miracles can teach; it is simply that our faith matures independent of these signs. We exult in the sheer *is-ness* of God. Our soul expands with a new depth of pure faith, hope, and love. Summarizing these graces, St. John says:

> As a result the soul enjoys divine and lofty knowledge by means of the dark and naked habit of faith; and the admirable delight of love through charity, by

which it rejoices in no one other than the living God; and satisfaction in the memory by means of hope. All of this is a splendid benefit, essentially and directly required for the perfect union of the soul with God (*AMC*, III, 32 [4]).

10

Joy of the Will in Spiritual Goods

(Book Three, Chapters 33 to 45 of the *Ascent*)

A good rule of thumb to remember while reading the *Ascent* is rearticulated in this section. It is that sensory satisfaction can detour our dynamic for transcendence. Spiritual goods refer to whatever motivates us to turn our minds and hearts to divine things, to stimulate conversation with God, to promote charity, and to place ourselves in a posture of receptivity to the self-communications of God.

St. John names two such classes of goods: delightful and painful. The latter will be treated only when he describes what occurs in the *Dark Night*, where clear and distinct knowledge of spiritual goods becomes vague and obscure. Even though the intellectual knowledge of God remains indistinct to the intellect, what is received by way of infused loving knowledge is in itself profoundly transforming. Here in the last chapters of the *Ascent*, St. John concentrates on "delightful" goods, clearly and distinctly understood, only hinting at those paradoxically painful yet wonderful touches that still preserve the mysterious transcendence of the Trinity.

There are, according to St. John, four kinds of goods that give distinct joy to the will and by extension give

169

rise to an understanding of God in the intellect through faith and in the memory through hope. He names these goods: *motivating* (the only category he completes, these being, statues, paintings of saints, oratories, and ceremonies); *provocative* (he devotes the last chapter of the *Ascent* to this category, then the text ends abruptly); *directive*; and *perfective*.

Statues, Paintings, Devotions. In regard to goods that motivate the soul to press onward in its journey to union with God, it is wise to recall why St. John is so cautious about basically good practices fostered by the church. It is due to his experience, to what he has witnessed in his role as a spiritual director. Many people simply stop at the level of sensory satisfaction, thinking that this is the essence of a motivating experience. They do not move through it to the level of spirit. The point is:

> Hardly will anyone be found in whom sensory satisfaction does not in some way spoil a good part of what was destined for the spirit, for senses drink up the waters before they reach the spirit, and thus leave the spirit dry and empty (*AMC*, III, 33 [1]).

This is hardly the intention of a *motivating* spiritual good. It is meant to propel the soul forward in the adventure of contemplative union, not to attach it to the surface meaning of things. Until the thread of attachment to a book or an image is cut, the solitary bird cannot soar free. Yet how many people are there in all cultures and ages who rejoice more in a painting of their favorite saint than in what the saint himself or herself stands for? How many wear a golden chain and cross around their necks for ornamentation without dwelling on what that symbol intends them to become?

Statues, says St. John, who must have been surrounded by them in Spain, are meant to awaken devotion, to motivate the will, to rouse the soul to reverence by means of them. They are, therefore, a *spiritual* good, not merely an earthly representation. Yet he has obviously met persons in quest of a deep life with God who center more on the elaborateness of the artisan's work than on the devotion a saint's life ought to call forth. One can admire a statue or painting aesthetically while remaining lukewarm spiritually! The idea is to direct interior devotion "toward the invisible saint in immediate forgetfulness of the statue" (*AMC*, III, 35 [3]), lest the love and joy of the will latch onto the sensual satisfaction and forego the spiritual orientation.

St. John is unquestionably upset by this distortion of devotion:

> Without any repugnance for vain worldly fashions, [some] adorn statues with the jewelry conceited people in the course of time invent to satisfy themselves in their pastimes and vanities, and they clothe the statues in garments that would be reprehensible if worn by themselves — a practice that was and still is abhorrent to the saints represented by the statues (*AMC*, III, 35 [4]).

From collecting figurines to "little more than doll-dressing" to the danger of idolatry, one risks distorting the true purpose of these pointers to the transcendent by confining their enjoyment to sensate pleasures and ignoring the call to charity. "As for devotion of the heart," adds the saint, "there is very little." The following example, involving the rosary, makes clear what St. John means:

> You will hardly meet anyone who does not have some weakness in this matter. They want the rosary to be made in one style rather than another, or that it be of this color or that metal rather than the other, or of this or that particular design. One rosary is no more influential with God than is another; His answer to the rosary prayer is not dependent upon the kind of rosary used. The prayer He hears is that of the simple

172 JOHN OF THE CROSS: THE ASCENT

and pure heart, which is concerned only about pleasing God and does not bother about the kind of rosary used (*AMC*, III, 35 [7]).

In contrast to the "vain covetousness . . . that clings to everything" (*AMC*, III, 35 [8]), the truly devout person passes quickly beyond the visible image to the invisible ideal it represents, conforming his meditation to that which transcends the finite and opens one to the infinite. Even if a favorite object of devotion, say a crucifix, is lost, one can let go of the disappointment because the Christ one adores lives within one's heart. The image inspires devotion, but if it is taken away, the loss is not that great.

What matters is to look upon the representation with the faith and purity of a prayerful heart devoid of hysterical or magical delusions. Over the years reports abound about weeping statues or moving eyes in marble figures to which the curious flock. This hunger for the spectacular is the opposite of the quiet devotion God might arouse in the heart of a sincere seeker, who, in beholding a figure, becomes motivated to a new depth of faith. The image is only an instrument God may use to enkindle in some people more prolonged prayer and devotion. Thus the work of the holy one represented, whatever the quality of the workmanship, continues to be efficacious for the whole church.

The same principle applies to pilgrimages to holy places. It is less the place itself and more the motivation and effort required to arrive there that inspires prayer and increases communion with God. Of course, the trip can be motivated mainly by the need for recreation. Where devotion is lacking, no trip or art treasure in itself can evoke it.

Our Lord was indeed a living image during His sojourn in this world; nevertheless, those who were faithless received no spiritual gain, even though they frequently went about with Him and beheld His wondrous works (*AMC*, III, 36 [3]).

St. John does acknowledge that the memory of an image that deeply affected a person may continue to have a supernatural effect. The repercussions of a visit to Lourdes or Fatima may stay with one for a lifetime. However, the same cannot be said of a powerful aesthetic experience, like the sight of Michelangelo's *Pieta* in St. Peter's. To recall its delicate craftsmanship may be accompanied by a feeling of devotion but what stimulates the will's affection may be due more to natural preference than to supernatural piety.

One has to be most cautious about so-called supernatural effects (movements, strange lights, explicit words) associated with certain replicas. While these may be destined by God to increase devotion, they may also be used by the devil to deceive the beholder and provoke a hoax. Because of these and other complexities, St. John proceeds to discuss practical ways in which we can avoid the errors and obstacles arising from images.

There is no doubt in his mind that the "prince of darkness" can transform himself into an "angel of light" (cf. 2 Cor 11:14) for the sake of deceiving a person too dependent on extraordinary phenomena manifested through images. The only solution is to purge our will of the thrill we find in this or that representation of the divine and direct our intentionality past the image to the imageless God. One maxim offered by St. John is sufficient to cover all cases:

> Since images serve as motivating means toward invisible things, we should strive that the motivation, affection, and joy of will derived from them be directed toward the living object they represent (*AMC*, III, 37 [2]).

The "active night of the will" refers to our capacity — indeed our decision — not to allow our senses to be so absorbed in an epiphany of the holy that we cease moving through the "accident" to the "substance," to the living and divine essence therein represented. This commitment saves us from delusion in three ways. We attend to the mystery behind the image, not its superficial manifestation; we do not stop at sense perception but proceed through it to worship of the living God; we do not place our trust in one image more than another but view all as vehicles God may use to disclose divine directives and draw us closer to union.

Oratories and Places of Prayer. Working as he did in many religious communities and understanding the human tendency actualized many times over in the history of the church to build more and more elaborate edifices for the sake of spreading the faith, St. John turns to the related subject of "oratories." Here is another realm where the sensual can overtake and absorb the spiritual, where visible objects can become more significant than their invisible source, where possessiveness and attachment can be justified in the name of preserving holy things.

An oratory in this sense can become a decorator's dream. Images are added here and there and adorned so elaborately that one could almost charge money for a visit. The problem is that people do not love God more solely because of the way their place of prayer is arranged. "Rather they love [God] less, since the delight they find in these ornate paintings withholds their attention from the living person represented" (*AMC*, III, 38 [2]).

The opposite extreme of a sloppy, unkempt place with no aesthetic sensitivity produces the same result of detracting one's attention from the divine. Where is our heart in all of this? That is the only important question. Do we celebrate God or our own clever designs or

lack thereof? Is our aim seeing or being seen or pleas-
ing God? Again what moves us to devotion? Consider
religious festivals, St. John says. Are they centered on
God's glory or on monetary gain and mere recreation?
The scandal of irreverences in gatherings organized for
God's service is clearly offensive to the saint:

> How many festivals, my God, do the children of men
> celebrate in Your honor in which the devil has a
> greater role than You! And the devil, like a merchant,
> is pleased with these gatherings because he does more
> business on those days. How many times will You say
> of them: *This people honors Me with their lips alone, but
> their heart is far from Me, because they serve Me without
> cause* (Mt 15:8–9) (*AMC*, III, 38 [3]).

What motivates us must be the love of God alone, not
what we feel or may derive from a worship service.

How, then, should we use oratories to direct our spirit
and our desire to adore God in them? The first rule is
to arrange these places so that they do not distract us
from prayer but provide a conducive atmosphere for
interior recollection and peace of soul. At the beginning of the spiritual life, it is likely that a seeker will
derive some sensible consolations from prayer in special places or from a certain object of devotion since by
these means God is weaning the soul away from mundane attachments toward a love for the divine mystery.
But to advance on this road, a time will come when we
must divest ourselves of sensory satisfactions and turn
our hearts wholly toward interior recollection and mental communion with God. When this happens it is surprising how quickly one can press the objects of sense
stimulation under the "cloud of forgetting" and move
upward into the "cloud of unknowing." At this stage
one may even become a bit of an iconoclast, prefer-
ring austere places to those that are ornate, finding in

barrenness a stark beauty. It is like the feeling of leaving picturesque cathedrals in Spain for the peace of a Carmelite monastery. Rather than concentrating on what stimulates us sensually or makes us feel comfortable aesthetically, we should prefer sites that facilitate interior stillness, sites freest from sensible objects, so that, unimpeded by any one thing, be it temple or mountaintop, we may adore God in spirit and truth (cf. Jn 4:20–24).

Statues, images, and oratories are not stopping points but starting places for inner devotion. We pray in the living temple that is our recollection of soul. We offer ourselves to God with a pure conscience, a heart full of love, with a will wholly obedient to God, a mind set upon God (cf. AMC, III, 40 [2]). It is for this reason that the scriptures recommend that we choose a solitary place (cf. Mt 14:23), one conducive to the transformation that must occur as we turn the joy in our will toward the invocation and glorification of God, paying no attention as such to exterior feelings of fulfillment. To the degree that we are bound to the delight of sensory devotion, we will never succeed in passing on to the sheer joy of spiritual communion in which all things are reclaimed in God.

Impediments to union will arise if we persist in remaining too attached to sensible gratifications sparked by the use of devotional objects and places. For one thing, St. John says, it will be impossible for us to reach inward recollection of spirit. This depends upon our willingness to let go of sensory delights. For another, we may find ourselves incapable of praying everywhere, unceasingly as St. Paul admonishes us to do (cf. 1 Thes 5:17), because we are overly dependent on places suited to our taste. It is like the person who always has to sit at the end of the pew. People have to crawl over her when the church is crowded because she refuses to slide toward the center. This is *her* place, and she guards it like a fortress. Such outer fortifications impede the kind of inner progress St. John is guiding us toward. We must be careful not to confine the great adventure of spirituality to one safe spot or to make the mistake of identifying "it" with a series of spots to which one has to travel constantly. The grass-is-greener mentality always breeds inconstancy, instability.

> Some never persevere in one place — nor even at times in one state — but now you see them in one spot, and now in another; now choosing one hermitage, now another; at one moment they will be decorating one oratory, and at the next, another (*AMC*, III, 41 [2]).

Some go so far as to change from one vocation to another, so entrapped are they in their own addictive needs for self-gratification. They can never settle down, recollect their minds, discipline their erratic wills, and suffer the discomforts of ordinary living for Christ's sake.

> Consequently, as often as they see a seemingly devotional place, or way, or state of life adapted to their disposition and inclination, they immediately leave what they have and follow after it. And since they are motivated by sensible gratification, they soon begin to look for something else; for sensible satisfaction is inconsistent and very quick to fail (*AMC*, III, 41 [2]).

Devotional places can promote faith, provided we know how to properly conduct our will in regard to them. For this part of the journey, St. John puts forth three suggestions. Being a lover of nature himself, as his poems attest, he recommends sites that offer pleasant variations in the placement of trees, in the flow of the land, and yet provide an occasion for solitude and quiet. Amidst the beauty of nature, one experiences the place as such fading into the background as the spirit moves inward to be wholly present to God.

A second place of choice for St. John is the wilderness. In a locality of silent splendor, God moves the will to love. One longs to return there, but soon discovers that it is not the place as such but God who grants the favor of graced intimacy. We can retire to the hermitage of our heart at any moment we so choose. Even being alone in our car on a long driving trip can become for us a desert experience. Even so, St. John recommends our returning once in a while to the wilderness as we know it (an actual desert, a deserted shore, a mountain retreat, somewhere away from it all) because we really praised God there; we thanked God from the bottom of our undistracted heart for these favors; we remembered the graces we have received and in us, busy as we are, fervent devotion was awakened. The desert can rekindle in hearts attached to worldliness the living flame of love. In the desert we know that in the end we have only God to go home to.

Thirdly, if our travel budget allows, it might be wise once in a while to pilgrimage to epiphanic places — the Holy Land readily comes to mind — where God walked and where, as on Mount Sinai, he chose to be invoked and worshipped. Again it is not the place as such, but the devotion aroused within, that matters. Because God hears us whenever and wherever we call, we can be in God's presence any time we approach the holy of holies with integral faith and no attachment whatsoever to sensual or spiritual gratification (cf. AMC, III, 42 [6]).

Ceremonies. The last "motivating means" prompting people to prayer are religious ceremonies, notably the liturgical. Here St. John speaks as a true reformer. He was well aware in his day of abuses in liturgical settings that supported not the purity of the eucharistic celebration but a number of superstitions displeasing to God.

These people attribute so much efficacy to methods of carrying out their devotions and prayers and so trust in them that they believe that if one point is missing or certain limits have been exceeded their prayer will be profitless and go unanswered. As a result they put more trust in these methods than they do in the living prayer, not without great disrespect and offense toward God (*AMC*, III, 43 [2]).

We also know from experience how fanatical people can get if too few or too many candles are lit, if the parish council dares to recommend a change in "their" Mass schedule, if certain prayers are not recited at the same time and in the same manner every day. Compulsiveness replaces relaxed contemplation. Indiscretion also abounds when people expect that at the end of such and such a ceremony their prayers and petitions will be answered in exact detail or that some great revelation will be disclosed to them. This tendency seems to point to an hysterical component — dangerous indeed because God may give "the devil permission to deceive them through an experience and knowledge of things far from profitable to their souls" (*AMC*, III, 43 [3]). Lacking is trust in God, which has been displaced by confidence in the ceremony or the recitation of multiple prayers solely to tempt God.

The best protection against either the compulsive or the hysterical extreme is to seek first and chiefly the reign of God and, as scripture assures us, all other goods will be added to this (cf. Mt 6:33). The path to follow, repeats St. John, is not to desire methods for their own sake but to pray with simplicity. The saint is sure that to "obtain an answer to the requests we bear in our hearts, there is no better means than to concentrate the strength of our prayer upon what is more pleasing to God" (*AMC*, III, 44 [2]).

We are always on safe ground if we remain faithful to the liturgy prescribed by the church and the way of prayer taught to us by Jesus. He gave his disciples the

Pater Noster (cf. Lk 11:1–4); he assured them that God
hears the prayers of our heart and gives us what is
fit and good for us (cf. Mt 6:7–8); he said our prayer
should never cease (cf. Lk 18:1). In fact, says St. John,
Jesus taught us only two ceremonies to use in prayer:
one was to pray in secret in our room (cf. Mt 6:6) or, if
not there, in the wilderness or in the quiet of the night
(cf. Lk 6:12). While not hesitating to approve customs
setting aside certain days for novenas, fasting, and like
devotional practices, St. John never wavers from his conviction that these methods can become more important
than the aim of carrying them out. Always the honor
belongs to God not to any set hour or practice of prayer.

Provocative Goods. The last chapter of the *Ascent* deals
with the second category of spiritual goods. It is easy
to imagine that St. John had to make a choice: to continue the in-depth analysis begun in his critique of "motivating goods" or to trust that by now we know the
principles of spiritual progress and can apply them ourselves. He must have sensed the limits of time, for he
had worked on this book already for six years from 1579
to 1585. He had to heed the voice of the Holy Spirit to
press on in the composition of his other great works.
Because he wrote from an already conceived synthesis
of the spiritual life, I believe it is safe to say that the
Ascent is complete by implication. Everything he has to
say in one way or another addresses the path to union
with God and the experience of divine intimacy. The
last chapter of the *Ascent* also introduces us in a special
way to the kind of teacher and preacher St. John must
have been. As we shall see, he sets a high standard for
this office.

Provocative goods arouse or persuade one to serve
God; hence this chapter addresses in particular preachers and what applies to them as well as what pertains to
their hearers. The preacher, above all, must be a model of

humility, shunning any trace of vain joy and presumption because this person is a messenger of the mystery hidden for ages but revealed in Christ Jesus (cf. Col 1:24–28). Preaching, therefore, is more a spiritual than a vocal expression. According to St. John, though this office is practiced through exterior words, its force or efficacy comes only from a properly disposed spirit.

> No matter how lofty the doctrine preached, or polished the rhetoric, or sublime the style in which the preaching is clothed, the profit does not ordinarily increase because of these means in themselves; it comes from the spirit of the preacher (*AMC*, III, 45 [2]).

A twofold preparation must occur if preaching and practice are to complement one another, if the communication is to be a word of power capable of converting hearts and advancing commitment to Christ. The preacher must prepare to teach and the hearer to listen. Preachers' words must flow out of their interior life; they cannot preach the law of God without making a life-long, sincere effort — despite human failings — to keep it. People will sense the disconnect between lofty words about God and a life that is too ego-centered to readily know God. Teachers of theology must believe and live the gospel message or their communication cannot be convincing to people. Listeners learn the most from lived experience, from sensing in the presence of the preacher the transforming power of God's word.

St. John is a believer in the principle that "the better the life of the preacher the more abundant the fruit, no matter how lowly his style, poor his rhetoric, and plain the doctrine" (*AMC*, III, 45 [4]). What enkindles fire are not empty words but a living spirit. However learned a preacher may be, it is to no avail if this knowledge is not at the service of self-effacement so God may shine forth. Good communication techniques (style, gesture, carefully selected phrases) when combined with good

substance are surely effective but unless these are accompanied by a good spirit, "the sermon," says St. John,
"imparts little or no devotion to the will."

He compares such a sermon to a musical concert: It
sounds lovely but it leaves the will as weak and remiss as
before. It does not move listeners to reflect on their lives,
to pray, to practice good works. Words are soon forgotten and a new, more exciting preacher is sought, if the
will is not incited to make more Christ-centered choices.

The listener by implication has to attend to the word
with more than sensory adherence to pleasant stories,
or effective delivery. Mental gymnastics may gratify the
mind, but they have no lasting effect upon the spirit. It is
not enough to praise the preacher. Real hearing implies
that we must be willing to amend our lives by means of
charity (cf. 1 Cor 2:1–4).

On that note so ends the *Ascent of Mount Carmel*. Like
John the Baptist, St. John of the Cross has prepared the
way for the Master, Christ Jesus, to enter our world. He
has taught us about the inner and outer dynamics of
formative spirituality and charted a trustworthy course
toward union with God from the first feeble steps to the
fullness of divine intimacy. The journey is far from over,
but at least we have made a serious start.

With this much of the road transversed, we can proceed into the dark night, the second part of the treatise, in which we shall behold as never before the pure
light of divine love through the grace of passive purification. May this companion to the *Ascent* encourage
you to continue reading the *Collected Works*. Most of all
may God grant you the grace to live in faith, hope, and
charity the timeless insights of a true spiritual master,
whose gentle promptings help all of us to find the way
to heaven's door.

Epilogue

I am aware that the *Ascent-Dark Night* must be read as one continual treatise on the spiritual journey leading to the "stilling of our house" in the center of God's consuming love. I hope in a second book to provide a companion to the *Dark Night*, but I wanted to complete this first volume as a tribute to St. John's genius in his 400th anniversary year, 1591–1991.

I trust that the line-by-line style of formative reading modeled in this book will encourage you to take every word seriously, to examine your hearts honestly, and to traverse courageously the road that leads to the summit of the mount. None of this is possible without the grace of God. I would like, therefore, to conclude this book with a poem I composed to thank God for gracing us with so fine a guide.

To St. John of the Cross
(1542–1591)

Put arid eloquence away
Leave worldly rhetoric behind,
So says the Spanish master,
"Bring God before your mind."

Be patient, understanding
Have love for humankind,
So says the Spanish master,
"Bring God before your mind."

I pondered long one night
With what words to respond,
"Love God alone and wholly,"
So says our dear St. John.

The message is so simple
So clear and so profound,

"Love God alone and wholly,"
So says our dear St. John.

My soul, embrace the darkness
Set your house at rest,
The Holy One awaits you
And brings to close your quest.

My soul, cling not to pleasure
Choose holiness instead
Choose nothing for its own sake
Save God whose way you tread.

Creator, Source of life,
Whose love sustains us all
How wondrous is the love
That overcomes our fall.

I saw God as the center
Of every living thing,
I knew God as my savior
In whom my soul can sing.

O gentle Spanish master
Your words resound in me,
Grant me the grace to answer,
"O God, my all for Thee."
                    — Susan Muto,
                    Segovia, Spain

Bibliography

Anonymous. *The Cloud of Unknowing and the Book of Privy Counseling*. William Johnston, ed. Garden City, N. Y.: Doubleday Image Books, 1973.

Athanasius, St. *The Life of Anthony*. Robert C. Gregg, trans. New York: Paulist Press, 1980.

Barnstone, Willis. *The Poems of St. John of the Cross*. Bloomington, Ind.: Indiana University Press, 1968.

Bendick, Johannes. "God and World in John of the Cross." *Philosophy Today*, 16 (Winter 1972), 281–94.

Benedictine of Stanbrook Abbey. *Medieval Mystical Tradition and St. John of the Cross*. London: Burns and Oates, 1954.

Brenan, Gerald. *St. John of the Cross: His Life and Poetry*. With a translation of his poetry by Lynda Nicholson. Cambridge: Cambridge University Press, 1973.

Brice, Fr. *Journey in the Night: A Practical Introduction to St. John of the Cross*. New York: Frederick Pustet Co., 1945.

———. *Spirit in Darkness: A Companion to Book Two of the "Ascent of Mt. Carmel."* New York: Frederick Pustet Co., 1946.

Bruno de Jesus-Marie. *Saint John of the Cross*. Benedict Zimmerman, ed. New York: Sheed & Ward, 1932.

Burrows, Ruth. *Ascent to Love: The Spiritual Teaching of St. John of the Cross*. London: Darton, 1987.

Campbell, Roy, trans. *Poems of St. John of the Cross*. London: Harvill Press, 1951.

Centner, David. "Christian Freedom and the Nights of St. John of the Cross." *Carmelite Studies*, 2 (1982), 3–80.

Clarke, John, trans. *Story of a Soul: The Autobiography of St. Therese of Lisieux*. Washington, D.C.: Institute of Carmelite Studies, 1975.

Crisogono de Jesus Sacramentado. *The Life of St. John of the Cross*. Kathleen Pond, trans. London: Longmans, Green & Co., 1958.

Criagono De Jesus, OCD. *The Life of St. John of the Cross*. New York: Harper and Bros., 1958.

Cugno, Alain. *Saint John of the Cross: Reflections on Mystical Experience*. New York: The Seabury Press, 1982.

Diken, E. W. Trueman. *The Crucible of Love: A Study of the Mysticism of St. Therese of Jesus and St. John of the Cross*. New York: Sheed and Ward, 1963.

Francis of Assisi. *Omnibus of Sources*. Chicago: Franciscan Herald Press, 1972.

Gabriel of St. Mary Magdalen, OCD. *St. John of the Cross: Doctor of Divine Love and Contemplation*. Cork, Ireland: The Mercier Press, 1947.

————. *The Spiritual Director According to the Principles of St. John of the Cross*. Benedictine of Stanbrook Abbey, trans. Westminster, Md.: Newman Press, 1950.

————. *Visions and Revelations in the Spiritual Life*. Benedictine of Stanbrook Abbey, trans. Westminster, Md.: Newman Press, 1950.

Gaudreau, Marie M. *Mysticism and Image in St. John of the Cross*. Frankfurt am Main: Peter Lang, 1976.

Hammarskjold, Dag. *Markings*. Leif Sjoberg and W. H. Auden, trans. New York: Alfred A. Knopf, 1969.

Hardy, Richard P. *Search for Nothing: The Life of John of the Cross*. New York: Crossroad Publishing Company, 1982.

Huxley, Aldous. *The Devils of Loudun*. New York: Harper, 1952.

Julian of Norwich. *Showings*. Edmund Colledge, O.S.A., and James Walsh, S.J., trans. New York: Paulist Press, 1978.

Kavanaugh, Kieran and Otilio Rodriguez, OCD, trans. *The Collected Works of St. John of the Cross.* Washington, D.C.: ICS Publications, 1979.

Kierkegaard, Soren. *Purity of Heart Is to Will One Thing.* Douglas V. Steere, trans. New York: Harper Torchbooks, 1956.

Lipski, Alexander. "Living the Truth of the Cross: Edith Stein and John of the Cross." *Carmelite Digest,* 2:2 (Spring, 1987), 43–47.

Lucien-Marie de Saint-Joseph. "Spiritual Direction According to St. John of the Cross." *Carmelite Studies,* 1 (1980), 3–34.

McCann, Leonard A. *The Doctrine of the Void: The Doctrine of the Void as Propounded by St. John of the Cross in His Major Prose Works and as Viewed in the Light of Thomistic Principles.* Toronto: Basilian Press, 1955.

Merton, Thomas. *The Ascent to Truth.* New York: Harcourt, Brace & Co., 1951.

_____. "Light in Darkness: The Ascetic Doctrine of St. John of the Cross." In *Disputed Questions.* New York: Farrar, Straus and Cudahy, 1960, 208–17.

Morneau, Robert F. "Principles of Asceticism," *Review for Religious,* 44:3 (May/June, 1985), 410–425.

Muto, Susan A. *Approaching the Sacred: An Introduction to Spiritual Reading.* Denville, NJ: Dimension Books, Inc., 1973.

_____. "Union with God through Faith." *Envoy,* 25:1 (January-February, 1988), 18–23.

_____. "Nothing — Only God." *Living Prayer,* 20:1 (January-February, 1987), 3–8.

_____. "Faith in the Cross: An Analysis of the Path Leading to Eternal Life in Book II of *The Ascent of Mount Carmel.*" *Mount Carmel,* 36:1 (Spring, 1988), 4–8.

_____. "The Call to Contemplation." *Mount Carmel,* 37:2 (Summer, 1989), 62–74.

————. "The First Stage to Union: The Active Night of the Senses." *Review for Religious*, 46:2 (March-April, 1987), 161–177.43–47.

————. "Lightness of Soul." *Carmelite Digest*, 4:3 (Summer, 1989), 16–22.

————. *Steps Along the Way: The Path of Spiritual Reading*. Denville, NJ: Dimension Books, Inc., 1975.

————. *The Journey Homeward: On the Road of Spiritual Reading*. Denville, NJ: Dimension Books, Inc., 1977.

————. *A Practical Guide to Spiritual Reading*. Denville, NJ: Dimension Books, Inc., 1976.

————. *Blessings That Make Us Be: Formative Living of the Beatitudes*. New York: The Crossroad Publishing Company, 1982.

————. *Pathways of Spiritual Living*. New York: Doubleday & Co., rpt. Petersham, MA: St. Bede's Publications, 1988.

————. *Meditation in Motion*. New York: Doubleday, Inc., 1986.

————and Adrian van Kaam. *Commitment: Key to Christian Maturity*. Mahwah, N. J.: Paulist Press, 1989.

Nims, John Frederick, trans. *The Poems of St. John of the Cross*. New York: Grove Press, Inc., 1959.

Peers, Edgar Allison. *Handbook to the Life and Times of St. Teresa and St. John of the Cross*. London: Burn Oates, 1954.

————. *Spirit of Flame: A Study of St. John of the Cross*. New York: Morehouse Gorham Co., 1944.

————. *St. John of the Cross and Other Lectures and Addresses 1920–1945*. Freeport, N. Y.: Books for Libraries Press, 1970.

Posiusney, Venard. *Attaining Spiritual Maturity for Contemplation According to St. John of the Cross*. Locust Valley, N. Y.: Living Flame Press, 1973.

Ryan, John K., trans. *The Confessions of St. Augustine.* Garden City, N. Y.: Image Books, Div. of Doubleday & Company, Inc., 1960.

Stein, Edith. *The Science of the Cross: A Study of St. John of the Cross.* Chicago, IL: Henry Regnery Co., 1960.

Stewart, R. H. J., SJ. *The Mystical Doctrine of St. John of the Cross.* New York: Sheed and Ward, Inc., 1934.

Teresa of Avila. *The Book of Her Life.* In *The Collected Works of St. Teresa of Avila.* Kieran Kavanaugh, O.C.D., and Otilio Rodriguez, O.C.D., trans. Washington, D.C.: Institute of Carmelite Studies Publications, 1976.

van Kaam, Adrian, C.S.Sp., Ph.D. *The Transcendent Self.* Denville, NJ: Dimension Books, Inc., 1979.

———. *Spirituality and the Gentle Life.* Denville, N. J.: Dimension Books, Inc., 1974.

———. *The Mystery of Transforming Love.* Denville, N. J.: Dimension Books, 1982.

———. *The Science of Formative Spirituality, Volume One: Fundamental Formation.* New York: Crossroad Publishing Company, 1983.

———. *The Science of Formative Spirituality, Volume Two: Human Formation.* New York: Crossroad Publishing Company, 1985.

———. *The Science of Formative Spirituality, Volume Three: Formation of the Human Heart.* New York: Crossroad Publishing Company, 1986.

Ward, Benedicta, trans. *The Sayings of the Desert Fathers.* Kalamazoo, MI: Cistercian Publications, 1975.

Wojtyla, Karol. *Faith According to Saint John of the Cross.* Jordan Aumann, trans. San Francisco: Ignatius Press, 1981.

———. "The Question of Faith in St. John of the Cross." *Carmelite Studies*, 2 (1982), 223–73.

Index